─ Walking My Walworth ─

A Sixties Childhood

MAGGIE FILKINS

authorHOUSE®

AuthorHouse™
1663 Liberty Drive, Suite 200
Bloomington, IN 47403
www.authorhouse.com
Phone: 1-800-839-8640

©2009 Maggie Filkins. All rights reserved.

No part of this book may be reproduced, stored in a retrieval system, or transmitted by any means without the written permission of the author.

First published by AuthorHouse 4/16/2009

ISBN: 978-1-4389-4818-8 (sc)

Printed in the United States of America
Bloomington, Indiana

This book is printed on acid-free paper.

No responsibility for the loss occasioned to any person acting or refraining from acting as a result of the material contained in this publication will be accepted by the author or publisher.

— Dedication —

This book is dedicated firstly to the memory of my Mum and Dad, and secondly to my brothers, sisters and my three daughters.

With special thanks to my husband David, daughter Lucy, sister Sandy and friend Barbara, for their constant support and encouragement, without which this book may never have been written.

Contents

Page

Dedication	v
Foreword	ix
Baptisms	1
Dad	3
Mum	9
Surrey Square	15
Country Dancing	21
Water Melon	23
Hopping the Wag	29
Buried Treasure	31
The Pictures	34
The Nicker Trilogy	36
i. *The Quick Fix*	*36*
ii. *Bare-faced Cheek! 2*	*38*
iii. *A Roll-on Parlaver.3*	*41*
The Crafty Drag	44
The Sixties Sweetshop	46
Pocket Money	48
Favourite TV Programmes	53
Culinary Delights	54

To see or not to see	58
Nitty Nora	61
Dressing Up	63
Unspoken	67
Playtime	72
Street Games	74
Wheels	84
Skipping an' Ball games	86
First Love	89
Milton House	94
Night Raiders	102
Hop-picking	105
East Lane Market	112
A Pub Crawl	115
Hard Up Options	120
The Money Lender	122
Provident Man	123
Homeworking	125
Runaway	128
Eviction	134
Author's note	145

~ Foreword ~

Most people know Walworth by association, i.e. the birth place of Charlie Chaplin and the East Street Market. The Walworth I knew and loved, growing up as a child in the sixties was quite different to the one I have recently re-visited as an adult. Come with me on a journey back into my childhood. This collection of 'snapshots', written from my childhood perspective, details everyday living and memorable happenings up until I reached the age of fourteen. At which point, due to unforeseen circumstances, everything changed, forever!

I encourage you to wake the child within yourself, take my hand and run with me, or if you prefer, "Get yer skates on mate." Experience the bombsites, the street games and playground songs. See the market as it was, the pubs and the pawnshops. Meet my family and friends and share in the Cockney-style humour, the hardships, the laughter and sadness, even the tears!

This is my story.

Maggie.

~ Baptisms ~

Back in the ole days, an' we're talking ancient here, when great grandma's had sixteen mouths to feed. Any ideas of material wealth were swept under the bed with the crumbs. Yet these great ladies managed to retain somefing plentiful and priceless. Their sense of humour.

They gave their darling daughters the cutest of names, like Fanny. 'Spect there were worse fings to be called, though none come to mind.

Apparently me great grandma made a huge blunder, by baptising me nanny as a double Fanny! Someone should have had the decency to explain, that Frances an' Fanny were one and the same.

I reckon that Vicar bloke, the little devil, was getting his own back to let that one go. Shortcomings in the collection plate maybe? who knows? But from that day on me nanny wore a thick skin. Kids sang songs about her. Not to be out-done, she made up her own versions too!

Conversations took on whole new meanings. Like when great grandma shopped at the local market and met with her friend by the fruit an' veg stall.

"So, said the friend, "Ow's yer Fanny doing then?"

"Ease up girls," said the ear-wigging stallholder. "Ain't respectable like, to be discussing such topic's in public. 'Nough to straighten me bananas."

"Ark at 'im. Cheeky young blighter," said Great Grandma. "Yer'll catch the back of me 'and quick as yer like." Grandma's hand became a skin covered mallet, or so I was told. Tangle with her an' your days were numbered. You were truly blessed if she larfed at your lip. But you sure as hell didn't mess with her Fanny.

So, when the stork delivers your girlie bundle, and you decide to revive some ancestral link, fink of me nanny an' her double whammy, an' name your little girl …Clare.

─ DAD ─

Let me tell you abaht me dad. If you'd have known him you would have loved him like I did. He was born in 1904 an' had one sister an' eleven bruvvers, although most of the bruvvers never survived infancy. He married Esther in 1929 an' they had two children, Florence an' Alfie. Dad's wife died soon after having Alfie, an' little Alfie himself died three months later. The toddler Florence was brought up by dad's mother in law. Although he fought hard to keep the child, the mother in law an' her army of relatives had ovver ideas, an' decided they were the best people for the job. Dad had no choice but to hand his daughter over. He left his home soon after an' became a Merchant Seaman. He worked as a Stoker an' a Cable Layer at sea.

When ashore, he loved nuffing better than Cockles for his tea on a Sunday. He was a brilliant darts player, an' if he fancied a pint at the local but had no money, he'd borrow 4d off his bruvver Stephen to get him through the door. Once in, he could stay all night if he wanted on the money made from throwing his darts.

He married me mum in 1951 an' became dad to her three young sons. Trying to get work close to home was tougher than he thought, people just didn't need Stokers in Walworth, so he took on a job as a Porter, working at Claridges. He met some famous people there, like Bob Hope, who he didn't like very much. An' he said of anuvver famous name, who he liked even less, "Wouldn't give yer the drippings of his nose, that one."

Dad eventually left to work for Courages in Tooley Street, as a Security Guard, mainly doing the night shift. Me an' little sister Sandy would sometimes sit in his hut by the main gates, all cosy an' warm with the electric fire glowing in the corner. Dad looking through his newspaper with his reading glasses ready to fall off his nose. We'd go on his rounds with him too, clocking in at some of the check points, before being sent off home. He was happy in his job, always smiling. It made him feel good, needed. Mum would send one of us down on a Friday night to pick up his wages. After taking out some pocket money for himself he'd hand over the little brown envelope.

Every year Courage's laid on a Christmas party for the staff's kids. There would be hundreds of us there! I remember queuing for me present at the end of the evening. I got a sweet shop which I wasn't too happy abaht so swapped it for Sandy's roulette wheel. Chances were I'd get to share the sweets anyway!

Dad was a typical Londoner, a family man, friendly, happy-go-lucky an' ready to help anyone out. Most mornings at six sharp he'd be knocking on the Baker's back door to buy us kids some mince for breakfast. He'd only buy five bits, one each, but the woman always chucked in anuvver piece, free of charge. Mince was like the stuff used for Christmas pies, only this version had some bread in too, an' had a paper thin pastry on top an' bottom. Us kids loved it.

Dad was my hero. King of the council flat or would have bin if his crown hadn't bin dislodged by his stepsons. Dad's downfall being that he was old, twenty years me mum's senior. Maybe the 'boys' thought that he weren't up to the job of keeping us young-uns in line? So Brian, mum's middle son, took over the job of chastising us kids when he thought it necessary. Dad never really stood a chance against mum's three strapping sons an' bit by bit he was pushed into the background.

His placid character kept the peace for most of the time, together with long hours spent in his bedroom, keeping out of the way. If he'd have bin younger an fitter, he might have knocked their blocks off, an' it would have served 'em right. Bet dad didn't fink like that though. He wasn't a violent man, never even had a proper row! The fact that he wasn't their dad was clear for all to see. He'd taken 'em on from when they were nipper's, brought 'em up like his own, an' for what? To become someone they joked abaht.

Mum didn't get off scott free neither. If she showed any wifely affection towards dad, her boys would larf at her, make her feel embarrassed. It was easier not to make waves. Mum an' dad still loved one anuvver though, I know, I'd seen the way they looked sometimes, almost like their eyes were smiling! He didn't need a suit weighed down with buttons, like the Pearly King who lived 'round the corner. Dad showed his worth by the fings he said an' done. 'Sides, he only had little legs, probably wouldn't be able to move much in such heavy, fancy trousers.

Memories of me dad are very bitty an' only really cover a short period. We were never in the same place at the same time for very long. When I came home from school I'd play out with me friends for a few hours, by which time dad had already left for work.

Dad was abaht five foot seven, an' had fick brown hair hidden by his flat cap. He always wore a waistcoat, indoors an' out. He loved to read the daily paper and Agatha Christie novels. Must have read the entire large print collection housed at the local library. I know, I used to get 'em for him, an' lug the damn fings home in a brown paper carrier. His black shoes shone like the star he was, plenty of spit an' polish an' a buffing cloth. Arf a rolled up fag often tucked behind his ear or hanging from the side of his mouth. If ever ash fell onto the mat he'd rub it in with his foot. "Keeps the moths out," he'd smile.

There are many fings abaht him that I should know an' don't. Like, what made him larf? Did he have a favourite colour? What were his hope's an' dreams? They surely had to be different to the one's he ended up with?

When I was twelve I was sent to the juvenile court for 'hopping the wag'. Dad came with me. We stood in front of the Judge while she debated with ovvers abaht what me future should be. Dad twiddled nervously with his flat cap, held tight in his hand. They wanted to cart me off to boarding school. Dad cried, pleaded with 'em, said he would take full responsibility for me. I cried too. Not for meself, but for me dad. He looked so sad an' it was my fault. It tore me apart to see him hurting like that. I fink the judge felt sorry for him too, since she let him take me home. Dad did 'is best by us kids, always, even when the 'boys' made it really tough for him. He wasn't scared to stick up for us neither. He would speak his mind, and often ended up paying dearly for it too. Like when the eldest boy, Charlie, lashed out, all cos dad asked if he could spare a chip from his plate for Sandy. Dad ended up on the floor, his back against the wall, crying. His face bruised an' his jaw broken.

His Daughter Florence would visit now an' then with her three sons, I reckon she was checking up on dad, making sure he was okay. Florence an' me mum used to be friends, but they had a falling out over somefing, I fink it was me dad. never found out for sure but it did makes fings difficult.

We did have some funny moments too, like the time when dad came to the hop farm for the weekend. Having found a pair of false teeth on the floor in the communal lavs, he rinsed 'em under the tap, an' went round the farm trying to flog 'em for 5s/6d. In the end he was happy to let 'em go for the bargain price of half a crown. Done deal. He was well chuffed. It gave me bleedin' nightmares for a week. Kept seeing this face grinning at me in me sleep with those bloody great 'nashers snapping up an' down.

An' the other fing clear in me head is the prank we played, as kids do. Me an' me sister Sandy found half a bag of flour in the otherwise empty food cupboard. We tipped it into one of dad's shoes an' propped it on top of his bedroom door, slightly ajar, so when he opened it he'd fink it was Christmas with snow an' everyfing. It never occurred to us that the shoe would clomp him on the head too. We peeked out from behind the coats hanging in the dark passage. What a mess! The stuff went everywhere an' dad was covered. We tried our hardest not to larf, we really did. He had a face like thunder. Lifting his arm to us he hollered, "Gertcha little bastards." We scarpered. One thing about dad was that he never, ever hit us. He'd raise his arm like he was going to. But the worse that happened was the "gertcha" (Cockney for, get out of'ere) was louder than the last time, an' could have given you earache. He had his own cure for that too. He would pop a bit of rolling tobacco in his mouth to moisten it, then pack the stuff in your ear. "That'll sort it," he'd say.

I understood abaht emotions an' such from an early age. Growing up in a family like ours provided a lifetimes experience in a short space of time. I was an "Old head on young shoulders," according to mum. I never told dad I loved him, never told anyone. There were unspoken rules about such fings. Still, I fink he knew. He loved us that's for sure. Sometimes I'd sit on his lap in the armchair by the fire, an' he'd whistle lovely tunes, like he did on the boats as a young Seaman. We weren't allowed to copy though, it was bad luck for females to whistle. He would cuddle us, make us feel special. Sometimes he'd sing too, but only when the 'boys' weren't 'round. His face would glow, like he was really happy in that moment. Just wish there had bin more moments like that.

All those lovey dovey words, the sloppy stuff, weren't part of our language, not like swearing. You couldn't get a sentence out without effing an' blinding. Wish I'd spent more time with me dad, talked more abaht anyfing an' everyfink. But you don't fink like that as kids, when your friends are bashing the street door down, trying to drag you out for a game of knock Down Ginger. Then, in the time it takes for a deep sob to hit the back of your throat, someone has flipped a switch an' it's all gone. Forever.

A joke told to me by me dad. "There were two Kings, which one had the baby?" Answer. Mrs King."

─ Mum ─

The large photograph tucked away in the sideboard drawer, was a portrait of mum aged seventeen. Her long brown hair rolled under in page boy style, shone like soft butter. The fitted Prince of Wales check suit (costume, as she called it) looked elegant an' expensive. She was beautiful.

In 1945 her Air Force Husband was killed in a plane crash, leaving mum with two young sons an' anuvver close to being born. She was just twenty one.

1951 was the year she married Alf, me dad. They lived in Blendon Row for a short time before moving to the nicer flats further along East Street, where us five young-uns were born. Bringing up eight kids on dad's Security Guard wages was never gonna be easy, but they managed.

People helped each ovver out. I'd offen be sent next door to borrow a cup of sugar or milk till payday. Sometimes I'd go over to Marie's, the local food shop, with a note asking for a couple of items to be put on the 'slate' till Friday. I fink mum stayed slim cos she never really bothered abaht food for herself. A cup of tea an' a fag was offen enough to keep her going.

She never ever moaned or complained abaht being short of money. She kept it to herself, hidden behind a smile or a joke. Whenever nan visited, she'd bring a couple of bags of shopping to help out, an' although mum never said, it was clear she saw herself as the poor relation. Her bruvvers an' sisters were all doing well for 'emselves, living in nice houses out in the country somewhere. They had all the modern gadgets an' stuff that money could buy, but never seemed to help mum out, not like the neighbours did.

If you can imagine a smiley, slim lady with bright blue eyes, larfing, joking an' dancing whenever she got the chance, that was me mum. She wore pencil skirts an' blouses an' high heels, (I liked clip-clopping abaht in them fings) 'cept of course when she was cleaning out the fire place, or scrubbing down the concrete steps in the flats. But she still looked lovely in her pinny an' headscarf. She was a smart lady who prided herself on looking nice. We offen wore a lot of secondhand clothes, mum too, but not just any ole rubbish. They had to look good an' have a lot of life left in 'em. I had some lovely frocks.

I fink if mum had to choose a favourite among her offspring's it would have bin Brian. He loved her to bits an' would show it by his constant teasing, an' going that extra mile to make her larf. Helped her out to, by taking us kids to 'Bonny's' in Peckham whenever we needed new clothes for family weddings an' fings. He'd put his hand in his pocket an' kit us out.

With mum being a superstitious lady, there were certain fings us kids became aware of. A bird flying into your home, or new shoes placed on a table were the ultimate in bad luck. Dropped cutlery had various outcomes too. Mum would never pick up a knife for instance, as this spelt trouble an' strife, a row with the husband. Crossed knives in a drawer would also bring abaht the same. A fork meant that a visit from the 'stork' was on the cards. She took no more chances with that one!

Our flat had three bedrooms but not enough beds, so us young-uns would top an' tail. In the winter mum would put coats on top of the blankets to keep us warm. Although the flat was crowded it was always an open house, an' no one ever got turned away. Like me older bruvver's friend, Alan, for instance. He came to live with us for a while cos he had no where else to go. He stayed for three years! A bit later on me big sister's friend moved in, with her kids too. We must have bin like sardines. Don't know how we managed, but we did.

Mum had a good sense of humour an' offen saw the funny side of most fings. One time we were walking home from the Old Kent Road, I was holding onto her arm as usual when suddenly a car nearby made the loudest bang ever! Mum screamed. Her shopping bag flew up the air. She thought she'd bin shot. When she looked down, her right leg was as black as a Coalman's neck. The car's exhaust had emptied itself all over her stockings. "Look what the bleeders done to me," she said, larfing with embarrassment. Taking the hanky from up her sleeve she rubbed it up an' down her leg, making it worse.

People were staring by now. Mum started waving her arm at the car driver stuck at traffic lights, mainly to show the on-lookers that she hadn't started out in such a state. "Ere, Guvner, she called. 'Ave a look at what yer've done to me." He zoomed off first chance he got. The assistant in the local shoe shop, let mum change stockings 'round the back. It made no difference, the black stuff had gone through the nylons an' plastered her skin. With a smirk on her face an' head held high, pretending she had no idea why people were pointing, we walked home.

When dad got sick an' gave up work, fings became more difficult. Mum would sing along to all the sad songs on the wireless, while doing the ironing. Her eyes all watery, you just knew that she was singing abaht her own life, an' that she wasn't as happy as she made out. Me an' me little sister Sandy wanted her to feel special, not just as our mum, but special as a lady dressed in smart suits, an' wearing the hats she loved an' wore as a young woman. We couldn't give her those fings but we thought of a way to help.

Whoever woke first in the night had to wake the ovver. We'd creep out of bed an' along the dark passage into the scullery. With a bowl of water, cleaning rags an' a bar of household soap, we'd clean that front room from top to bottom, finishing off by washing the lino, before sneaking back to bed. We couldn't wait to get up in the morning an' see the look on mum's face. We'd planned to do this once a week, but rarely woke up before daylight, by which time mum was already up an' doing.

I raced home from school one lunchtime, to get me plimsolls for the afternoons P.E lesson. Pulled the key out from behind the letterbox an' let meself in. There was no sound in the flat. Someone had to be home cos I could smell the smoke. Opening the front room door, I got the shock of me life! There, standing by the fire was me mum an' sister Rosie, just staring at each ovver. Arf the room was black with soot. They were covered in the stuff. Mum gave her head a gentle shake, an' a fick cloud fell onto her shoulders. All three of us fell abaht larfing as they tried to explain, that while warming their feet 'round the fire, the chimney decided to clean itself. Soot gushed out like water from a pulled lavatory chain. Too stunned to move they just sat there an' took the brunt of it. I reckon anyone else would have cried at having to clean up the mess, but not me mum. She thought it was hilarious, it tickled her for ages.

She did have some funny expressions, sometimes she'd say fings just to get you smiling. If any of us kids were slommaking abaht, going nowhere fast, she'd tell you to get a move on, "Yer're like a tit in a trance," was one of her favourites. An' if I walked into a room without me vest on, she'd say, "Put yer aligobs away girl, yer'll poke me eyes out in a minute." Even though I was as flat as a pancake.

Ovver times she'd make you larf till you cried with her risk taking. Like the afternoon she walked along with me to school. I was thirteen at the time. A young male builder walked in front of us, wearing nuffing but shorts. "Shouldn't be allowed, walking abaht like that. 'nough to give someone an 'eart attack." she said, jokingly. "I'll slap his arse, teach him a lesson." Cringing at the thought, I try to steer her past him, but she wasn't having any of it.

Within reach, she whacked the builder's bum. He jumped round, arms out to clout someone. "It's alright mate," said Mum, putting a hand up to calm him. "There was a bee on yer shorts. I was just getting rid of it for yer."

"Oh Thanks girl," said the builder.

"Yer welcome son," smiled Mum, wickedly.

Mum *was* special, she might not have thought it herself, but she was. Everyone loved her, especially dad, but for various reasons their love for each over was offen hidden. It could have bin so different for them, if only …

Playground Rhyme

One, two, three, Muvver caught a flea,
put it in a teapot an' made a cup of tea.
The flea jumped out, Muvver gave a shout,
Father came in with his shirt hanging out.

Surrey Square

"If you insist on acting like a baby, then it's only right that I treat you like one," said Miss Champagne, the Headmistress. She disappeared into her office an' returned with a camp bed. She set it up, bang in the middle of the hall an' ordered me to lie on it. Pushing a dummy in me mouth an' a teddy under me arm, she left. I liked everyfing abaht Surrey Square School, even Miss Champagne. I remember her as a round lady with dark wavy hair and a big lap, for bending kids over to give their bum a good smacking.

One Christmastime I sat cross-legged next to the giant tree, decorated with twinkling coloured balls an' fings. All the infants were there, listening to one of her speeches. Suddenly, a ball fell off, all on it's own, just plopped itself down beside me. I know I didn't touch it. "You there," Miss Champagne pointed at me. All the kids turned an' stared, like I'd got two heads or somefing. "Come here this minute." I laid across the rosy pattern on her baggy skirt, she lifted me frock an', whack! Went back to me place, scared to breathe even, 'case anuvver one plopped off. I wasn't a bad girl, mostly shy, but I did seem to get into trouble a lot.

The Headmistress had two babies of her own in school, Peewee an' Rusty, her sausage dogs. They followed her everywhere, plodding along behind like mini deputies. We pretended we liked 'em, but we didn't really. They were boring, never did anyfing.

At break time we'd drink our bottle of milk, then tear across the playground to the swings. Sometimes I stood for ages waiting me turn, but the girls wouldn't share, no matter how loud I 'uffed an' puffed. Then the bell went an' I'd lost me chance. That made me fed up. On rainy days we stayed inside reading comics in the hall.

Alfie an' Rosie, me bruvver an sister, were in the juniors. Their classes were upstairs, I'd be joining them after the summer holiday. That scared me. "Nuffing to worry abaht," said Mum. "Any problems yer go an' find Rosie. She'll look out for yer." Rosie was good at fighting, best girl fighter in school, everyone knew that.

During the holidays the school opened as a play centre. Us kids were always there, skipping, playing rounders an' ovver running games. There were dolls an' prams, everyfing you ever wanted. We'd do painting too. Big sheets of paper pegged on the easel. Brown rubber aprons that I couldn't stop sniffing, I like the smell almost as much as dad's boot polish, or the germolene mum plastered on me cuts an' grazes.

Had belly ache the morning of the new term. I didn't want to be a junior. 'Sides, they never had swings in their playground, just a white painted hopscotch for all the kids to share. "Yer'll be okay. I'll look after yer," smiled Rosie.

Mr Chaplin the Headmaster was skinny like mum, an' smiled a lot too! We sang hymns an' said prayers in assembly. One minute we're sitting then standing then sitting again, like jack in the boxes. I never knew the words to anyfing, so just moved me mouth, pretending. Then it was off to class with the new teacher.

In the first three years I became a good reader an' learned joined up writing. I did geography an' history an' knew all abaht the Kon Tiki expedition. In the playground I could hula-hoop an' skip, with bumps at the end! An' I played two balls up the wall better than most. But the fing I looked forward to more than anyfing was the dinner. I loved school dinners. Just a whiff of that food made me belly grumble like a plughole. Us hard-up kids got free meals. Each day we were given a small brass disc that we handed to the dinner lady, 'cept for the times when me an' Sandy popped 'em in our mouth, did handstands up the wall an' swallowed the bleedin fings. We still got a meal though. Puddings were best. Spotted dick, chocolate sponge an' treacle pud, all with fick custard that had even ficker skin. Once everyone had bin served we could queue for seconds. I was up there like a shot.

When Rosie an' Alfie both left for the senior schools, I had to learn to fight me own battles. Didn't like fighting, never really practised so wasn't any good at it. I had all the cheek an' daring when me family or friends were 'round, but on me own I was shy, an' stayed in the background.

The fourth year was a difficult time, hardly anyone in class spoke to me, an' the boys never wanted to partner me for country dancing neither. I never knew why, an' no one ever told me. I did have friends in the ovver classes though. Tim, who sat at the front of my class, was poor an' ignored too. We never spoke either. His mum came to school once an' I couldn't stop staring. She looked like a film star standing there outside Mr Chaplin's office. Her face all painted up an' she had big white sticky out hair. She wore a fur coat with dot shapes all over, like the cats on the telly. Tim ran up to her for a cuddle, but he didn't get one. She told him to pull his jumper down over the tear in his trousers instead.

Me an' Liz sat together. She was different from the ovvers. We became best friends an' went everywhere together. She had a posh house with carpets an' a washing machine, even a plug in iron! Mum would have liked a house like that. I slept over there sometimes. Her mum let me wear the spare school dress, blue an' white check with a little collar. Felt special in that. One day, Lizzie's aunt came over from Australia. She didn't have children, an' wanted to adopt me, take me back with her. It would have bin nice but I couldn't go, I'd have missed me mum too much.

Spent anuvver morning on the camp bed in the infants hall, for getting caught on the swings. Funny this time though, cos I could make faces at Liz down the ovver end in her own camp bed, dummy shoved in her mouth an' rocking her teddy to sleep. We were a sight better off than the poor sod walking abaht with a card tied 'round his neck saying 'I KICK'.

Never set out to make trouble for meself, it just sort of happened. Like in the art lesson when I spilt a drop of paint on Liz. The stand-in teacher went barmy. He painted me face, arms an' legs in front of everyone, then sent me out to wash it off. A lady helper outside the class tried to take me into the cloakroom to clean me up. I ran off, heading for the stairs. "I'm going 'ome to show me Mum, see 'ow he likes that," I shouted, through me tears. "She'll 'ave his guts for garters."

Miss Burns the English Teacher gave me lots to fink abaht. Not only was she lovely an' kind, but when she told one of her stories no one spoke or sniffed or moved. She didn't read from a book, she made 'em up as she went along. Me favourite was abaht some children going into a 'ghost' sweetshop after the war. I looked forward to those lessons every week. Miss Burns made me want to be a writer. I couldn't wait to grow up and get started. I already loved books, an' spent lots of time at the new library on the corner of East Street. The bright coloured covers always tempted me first. I had to read those stories, be part of that excitement hidden in those pages. I'd sit in the children's section for ages, sometimes till closing.

Last Christmas morning I woke extra early, grabbed the pillarcase from the end of the bed an' emptied it out. An orange, apple, some shelled nuts, a few sweets an' two books, Treasure Island an' Robinson Crusoe. I ran me hands over the shiny new covers, flicked through the nice clean pages, but I never read 'em, not once. Couldn't risk spoiling 'em, cos they were different, special. They were mine!

It was almost time for us fourth years to leave Surrey Square and go onto the senior schools. I'd only just turned eleven, so was one of the youngest. Most kids wanted to go to the mixed school in Mina Road. I didn't want to go anywhere. I was happy where I was. If I felt sick in the morning an' got sent home, I'd be back through those gates for the afternoon's lessons. It could never be the same somewhere else.

Liz had chosen the all girls school, Silverthorne. I decided to go with her since she was me only real friend. Of all the kids in Surrey Square there were only a handful going there. They were bound to keep us together, we didn't *know* anyone else. Sitting in that hall, fingers crossed so tight it hurt, we listened for our names as they read out the class lists. Me an' Liz had bin separated. From that moment on everyfing changed. On the outside I smiled, pretending it was okay, but it so wasn't. Inside I cried. I didn't wanna be on me own. Scared as hell an' hadn't a clue what to do abaht it.

Most of the kids in class lived in the same area, they were friends already. There was a group of loud mouth show-offs, who took the mick an' made you look stupid, just to get a larf. Not only that, they were huge, some twice me size. Our room was at the end of the corridor, opposite the cloakroom an' stairwell. I offen thought of escaping down those stairs, out that gate an' home. Never chanced it though, frightened of getting caught. Until one Monday morning…

Dressed in me navy uniform, mum unravelled the plaits in me hair. I was always nagging her abaht the length, an' how it never grew much past me shoulder. I had dreams of it hanging down me back an' swishing when I walked. Mum said that plaiting the hair made it grow quicker. I looked in the mirror at the funny wobbly strands. As she combed it through it got bigger an' bigger, like a frizz-ball. I hated it. "I'm not going out looking like this," I said, in a state of panic. Mum damped it down with water. It flattened some of the frizz, but still looked a mess.

The kids in class larfed out loud an' made fun of me. If I was more like Rosie, I would have beaten 'em up, all of 'em. See how they larfed then? That wasn't gonna happen, cos I couldn't really stand up for meself, not against a group anyway. One on one an' I might have given it me best shot, like when the boy in the flats spouted off abaht me family. Couldn't let him get away with that!

I went an' hid in the cloakroom. The girls piled out the doors to change classes. Soon as the corridor went quiet, I left. Ran from that place as fast as me legs would carry me, an' never ever entered that classroom again …

Country Dancing

I was that little girl left standing on her own. No one ever snatched *my* hand to dance. Not even Soapy Jimbo, so-called cos of him needing a good wash.

"Ain't dancing with her Miss," He'd say. "Rather drown meself."

I'd stand by the wall, twiddling me fingers an' biting me bottom lip. I wanted to cry an' clobber him one at the same time. Jimbo said stuff just to make ovvers giggle, an' maybe get some friends but it never worked. We didn't really fit in with the popular kids. Me an' him were similar, but with one obvious difference. He was a smelly ole git an' I wasn't. An' I'd rather eat worms than dance with him, so there!

If Miss picked someone for me, they'd protest loudly, so their mates would feel sorry for 'em instead of taking the mick. Fing is, I wasn't that bad. I had some nice frocks. Me fick brown hair was always shinning, an' I smiled a lot too.

I decided to take action an' better me chances of getting a partner. So, I prised a pink bow off me 10th birthday card, stuck me fringe back with mum's clips, an' popped the bow on top of me head. I thought I looked the best fing since, well, sliced bread I s'pose.

Country Dancing, what was that all abaht anyway? They didn't do that down the pub on a Saturday night. I wanted to learn proper stuff, like 'Knee's up Muvver Brown' an' 'Lambeth Walk,' not keep twirling under kids arms an' clapping an' stuff. 'Sides, they might dislodge me hair-do, scupper me Princess Status then where would I be?

Truth is, I *did* like country dancing. The music made me feel happy. It was fast an' fun an' I couldn't help but grin even when I knew I should be miserable.

A new boy called Richard started at the school. He spoke proper, like he was posh. His dad was an actor on the telly, a bit la-di-dah, mine was a Watchman at the brewery. He didn't talk posh, but it didn't matter cos he was already the best dad in the world.

Anyway, Richard was nice an' all the girls loved him, me too. Everyone wanted to be his friend. The pretty girls in their even prettier frocks stuck to him like bubble gum. I saw him looking at me a couple of times. He even smiled! He'd only bin at school a week an' he picked me for his partner. He wasn't threatened with the ruler, or dragged by the hair, screaming. He walked over all by himself an' took me hand, an' he didn't wipe pretend poo down his trousers neither. Must have bin the bow that did it?

Girls faces suddenly screwed up like dogs bums, an' drop-dead stares bounced off me like rubber darts. An' d'you know what? Nuffing could touch me that day. I grinned till I thought I'd get lock-jaw, an' I shone like the brightest, brightest shilling.

The nobody had at last become a real person, named Maggie. On account of that being me name.

—Water Melon—

"Don't go an' leave me on me own," I cried, arms stretched across the passage trying to block Alfie from reaching the door. "Won't be arf hour for gawds sake. What's up with yer lately?" he asked. "Yer're like a bloody water melon." He stood on the landing. The street lamps shinning in the fading light. Couldn't tell him, couldn't tell anyone. "Someone'll be 'ome soon, an' I'll be back in a little while. Just keep the door shut. Yer'll be ok." Alfie pounded down the stairs.

Everyone knew the lock was dodgy. You only had to lean on the door an' it opened. Sometimes we even put a sock in the door to keep it shut. Sitting on the bare floor I pressed me back against it, and waited. Where was everyone? Didn't they know I was on me own?

I never used to be such a scaredy cat. I'd play out on me own sometimes, skating round till after dark. It never bothered me. Mums probably 'round a neighbours, I decided. Cooing over me baby sister, four months old, with a little turned up nose like the rest of us.

Started finking abaht Jesus, and the messages on the book marks they gave me at Sunday School round Surrey Square. "You just ask and he'll help you," the teachers told me. Well I did ask, an' I fink he heard me 'cos no baby had popped out me belly button yet! Some of me mates said you only had to kiss a boy an' you'd get a baby. Me sister Sandy was found under a stall down the Lane, Mum teased. I never knew how babies got in your belly but I knew they came out through your belly button.

The ovver mission hall called Christways was at the top of Beckway Street. We used to go there sometimes an' play skittles. I was a bit too old at ten, since it was mainly for smaller kids, but they let me in just the same. Sometimes we'd sit in tiny curved back nursery chairs while the helpers read stories. I liked it there. One day the bulldozers came an' knocked most of the place down, along with the crumbling houses 'round it, creating anuvver bombsite.

It had just started to get dark. Me an' me mate John were playing in the park by the flats. A man walking by called out to us. He looked upset. We climbed over the railings an' went to talk to him. "I've lost my son," he said, an' described a thin, ginger haired boy. "Took his puppy for a walk, ages ago. Have you seen him?"

"We ain't seen anyone round 'ere Mister," said John. We went to climb back into the park.

"Can you help me find him? I'll give you half a crown each for your trouble." We didn't want to but the man just went on an' on. Me an' John walked off together.

"Best if we split up," the man called. "More chance that way." It didn't feel right, but I changed directions and the man walked behind me. A conversation started up in me head.

"Climb over the railing and run 'ome," said the little voice.

"I can't. I'm scared."

"Climb over…

I glanced up at the flats. Two sets of railings an' a grassed area between me an' safety.

"I can't. I'm scared." There was no one on the balconies, no one to call to. I carried on down Elsted Street past the fish shop.

"Let's try round there," he pointed to the right. What was the matter with me? Why didn't I just run off? The little voice continued its nagging in me head. "But he might catch me an' 'urt me." I answered.

We came upon a dark walkway with high wire fencing either side. I noticed a large, gaping hole on the left, big enough to climb through. "Sometimes my boy builds a camp here," he remembered. "He could be there now?"

The bombsite was quiet an' dark. There *were* camps there! He wasn't lying. He called his sons name. No answer. The wall at the back of the site was the remains of Christways Mission. With me back against the bricks, he explained abaht teenagers an' fings they got up to. He put his hand up me frock to show me. Tears streaming down me face, trying not to cry too loud cos it was making him mad. He laid his overcoat down in the dirt and pushed me onto it. Three older boys walked along the alleyway, chatting an' larfing. I turned me head towards 'em, hoping they would hear me sobs, an' come to help. The man clamped his hand across me mouth.

"If your mum and dad found you dead, they'd be really upset now, wouldn't they?" All the while he was doing this stuff, bad stuff. He took his winkle out. "I know your mum and dad."

"What, Clare an' Alf?" I answered tearfully.

"Yeah, know where you live too." He rubbed 'is winkle all over me, down there!

It suddenly dawned on me that this was it. This is how ladies got fat bellies.

"Don't let me have a baby, please Jesus. Mum's just had one, she couldn't cope with anuvver." I prayed loud in me head, over an' over.

Eventually, the man got up an' pulled out a handful of watches from his pocket. "I'll come up to your flat at nine tonight. I'll give one of these to your mum for you, for helping me out."

He was gonna let me go home.

"You mention this to anyone, and I'll come and get you. Do you hear me?"

I tried to run across to the fencing but me legs wouldn't work properly. They felt weak an' fuzzy, making me trip an' fall. Have to move faster before he changes his mind. Back to the fish an' chip shop now, nearly home.

Pushing open the street door, I crept along the passageway an' climbed into bed. Almost nine! Still dressed, I hid beneath the blankets, straining to hear the telly in the front room. When the programme changes it'll be time. He knows where I live. He's gonna knock the door. Waiting, listening, sobbing quietly, nothing! I wet the bed.

The next morning John came knocking. "You coming out?" he asked.

"Not yet, just got up."

"Did yer find that boy last night?"

I shook me head.

"What abaht the money then, did yer get it off him?"

"No, forgot."

John was staring like he didn't believe me. "'Ow come he was following yer," he asked.

"E wasn't," I snapped back, "'e went a different way." I shut the door an' went to snuggle by the fire, alone with me thoughts.

Fings just didn't make any sense. Boys liked their winkles; I knew that, cos they harped on abaht 'em offen enough. But why would anyone want to do scary stuff with somefing they peed out of? One boy in the flats was forever tricking the girls into touching his. "Want a sweet?" he'd say. "They're in me pocket, help yerself." I remember dipping into that pocket, once. Didn't find a sweet though, just a little warm spongy fingy poking through the lining.

Somefing else confused me too, like when boys called out to a girl, "Ere darling, fancy a bunk up?" They'd push their hips forward an' pull stupid faces. I'm sure this had to do with winkles as well. But what did it mean? Fing is, I gave Sandy bunk up's lots of times, by letting her stand on me hands an' lifting her up over the railings. I pulled faces too, but only cos she weighed a fuckin' ton!

Anyway, everyfing had changed. Me sisters didn't like to sleep with me anymore. They would wake up wet an' cold! I didn't do it on purpose, it happened when I was asleep. Got fed up keep going to the bagwash shop though, lugging that pillarcase filled with dirty clothes an' bedding. Even worse if you had to go back an' collect it later, still damp, an' weighing a ton. Me an' Sandy would drag it part way along the pavement. By the time we reached home, the bottom of the pillarcase looked grubbier than the scabby dog that scavenged our bins. Mum draped the washing over chairs an' dried it off in front of the fire.

The dark scared me too. Still played out with me mates, but never stayed out on me own. If I had to go on an errand I'd cry me eyes out, trying to persuade 'em to send Sandy instead. Me family thought I was having a strop or being lazy, they didn't understand the carry-on, an' I couldn't tell 'em, cos of what might happen. I'd end up running so fast there an' back, that it hurt to breathe.

I became a different Maggie, one with a secret that I couldn't share.

"'Ow come yer're always crying?" asked Alfie one day. "Yer're turning into a proper water melon."

"Don't like the dark, that's all."

"Since when?"

I shrugged me shoulders. Alfie offen called me water melon after that. I didn't mind 'cos he said it in a nice way, and he still looked out for me. He'd always be my bestest bruvver.

Hopping the Wag

When me an' Sandy clapped eyes on the blue Mini Minor in East Street, we were off. Little legs moving faster than the bargains at the market. We'd climb over the railings 'round the park area, an' take the short cut alongside the pram sheds, up the stairs of the flats, an' 'Bob's yer Uncle.' Indoors. Safe.

The School Board Man banged that door knocker like he was the Old Bill. We ignored him, till he got fed up and slung his hook. He'd squeeze all his fatness back into the Mini, an' drive off in search of some other poor sod.

We didn't play truant back then, we 'Hopped the Wag.' Secondary School had always bin a problem for me, I hated it. Sometimes me and me little sister would visit old Mrs Cole, losing her marbles a bit, but she liked a chat. 'Sides, her prefab was warm, and she always had cake!

"Like I ain't got enough to worry abaht," Mum would say. "Get yerselves out of her kitchen an' off back to school." But mum was too nice, too soft. We kids got away with a lot more than we should have. I fink the school board man worried mum. The idea of getting into trouble bothered her, but she never let on. Her real thoughts were always hidden behind a lovely smile. She jokingly nicknamed him Airball, but only for our benefit. She was always nice to his face though.

Sometimes he'd be sly, knock the door quietly an try to catch you out. I'd ease back the net curtain, just enough for one eye to peek through, an' look along the landing. Too late! He'd seen me. "Go away, we're not in," I'd shout.

This day he caught us off guard, though we spotted him just in time. Our little legs were off an' running. Up the stairs of the flats, an' screaming through the letterbox. No one home. No key.

Sandy stood on me linked hands, ready for a bunk-up to the fanlight window, high above the door, barely wide enough, but open. Part way through, an' I shoved her with all me might. I had visions of her zooming through that gap like Batman, an' ending up sliding down the passage wall. No such luck! "I'm bleedin' well stuck" she cried, "Me frock's caught on the latch,"

Arf in, arf out, going nowhere. Legs dangling like some trussed up turkey. "Ere, where d'yer get them new drawers?" I said. We were done for.

The fat man appeared and stood there, gawping, surveying the scene like that copper bloke on Dixon of Dock Green. "What's she doing up there then?" he asked, eyebrows disappearing beneath his messed up Beatle haircut.

Had to be careful here, get him on side if I could. I gave the sweetest, most innocent of smiles, sure to warm the cockles of his heart, an' in me bestest girlie voice I whispered, "Homework."

Buried Treasure

The old girl would chase you off that bombsite, screaming and yelling and cursing like she'd got earwigs up her bum or somefing. I swear she ran faster than Popeye's fancy woman, Olive Oil.

She scared me. She had a funny gob, no teeth, so her lips curled backwards. Gawd knows what she'd do if she caught up with you. "Probably mince yer up an' bung yer in a pie," at least that's what me big sister Rosie said.

Me little legs going ten to the dozen. I stretched out me hand for Rosie to grab an' pull me along, make me feet move faster, but she was up an' over the fence with our mates, an' yelling for me to get a bloody move on.

"The Witch is gonna get yer," chanted me sister's friend. Tears streaming down me face, an' nose running, straight onto me sleeve like magic. I jumped on that fence an' started climbing up. Friends jeering me on and Olive Oil getting closer an' closer …

Bombsites an' derelict houses lured us kids like a whiff of Pease pudding an' faggots. Just couldn't get enough of 'em. The site, alongside the flats had two entrances as far as we were concerned. Either the tall wire mesh fencing which separated the flats from the rubble. Or, through the garages, a short walk round the block, and there it was, open access. We always went for the easy option, the fence!

We'd play for hours at being Mums an' Dads, outlining the rooms for our makeshift house with bricks from the site. We each had our own role to play. I *never* got to be mum. I was too young. But I did get to make meat pie, by stirring dirt an' stones together in an old dented saucepan that someone had dug up earlier.

In the far corner of the bombsite stood the last couple of terraced houses, one empty, with its end wall showing two levels of peeling, patterned wallpaper. The upstairs open fireplace with its large black mantle looked strange just hanging there. "Yer'd need a bloody long poker to stoke that fire," Rosie teased.

The end house near the school wall is where the old girl lived. Someone was s'posed to move her out to a new place, 'cept it wasn't ready. We didn't mind her being there, on our bombsite. We didn't bother her neither, 'cept when she ranted on an' chased us all over the place. Made me legs ache! So, we'd get a bit lippy sometimes, but she started it first. Always!

This particular day I dug up real treasure, a pile of thrupenny bits. I wanted to tuck 'em in me pocket, keep 'em to meself, but I was that excited I told me sister. She shared 'em out. Her an' her friend Janie had the most cos they were older. I got one pocksey thrupenny bit, cos I was too young and young-uns didn't need much money. Wish I'd kept me gob shut.

So, there I was, done with the running and climbing up the fence. At the top I sat me bum on the fat post, ready to jump an' for Rosie to catch me. The old girl banged on the wire. I just knew she wanted to suck me bones with them gums. I needed a poo, bad. Me clothes were caught in the little sticky up bits of wire mesh. I couldn't free 'em, so Rosie jumped up, grabbed me feet and yanked me down. A bit of me frock was left hanging on the fence an' flapping away like a little flag.

I dug deep in me pocket for the thrupence, gone, fallen out on the wrong side of the fence. The old girl picked it up, spat on it to shift the dirt, and stuck it in 'er own pocket. Bleedin' cheek.

Peering through the mesh, fingers curled over the wire diamonds, I watched her walk away. I wasn't happy. Me mouth was arched like a pink rainbow. If mum had seen me she would have said, "Is that yer own face girl? Yer know if the wind changes it'll stay like that forever?" I did know, an' I didn't care.

I'd lost me treasure, an' me bestest frock now had a bloody great hole in. I was a miserable, humpy mare with a draft up me back. I told me sister that nuffing less than a toffee apple, covered in coconut bits would make me smile again, ever!

The Pictures

Saturday mornings were always exciting, providing we had a tanner (sixpence) to go to the Pictures. The ABC at the Elephant an' Castle was always packed out with screaming, yelling kids. It was never just about watching the films. You got to meet up with your mates, an' make as much noise as you wanted, without some grown-up breathing down your neck, and telling you to shut your cakehole. Some compare bloke would jump on the stage an' read out birthdays, and there was always a competition to enter as well. Me bruvver Alfie won the prize once for the best colouring skills! 'Cept he didn't do it, but I wasn't allowed to tell anyone that. He won a crate of Corona fizzy drink. Trying to carry that fing all the way home from the Elephant, nearly killed us!

We had to sing the ABC song as loud as we could before the film started. It's a wonder we didn't bring the roof down. Saturday mornings were the *bestest*!

"We are the boys an' girls well known as,
we are the minors of the ABC.
An' every Saturday we line up
to see the films, we like to shout aloud with glee.
We like to larf an' have a sing song
Just a happy crowd are we.
We're all pals together.
We are the minors of the ABC."

The Nicker Trilogy

Who'd have thought that me drawers, or lack of 'em, would have so many memories attached? It's not like we're talking heirlooms here! At best they were thick navy cotton. At worst, well, read on…

The Quick Fix 1

8 years tall. Vest tucked in me baggy drawers, which would have doubled as ankle warmers if it weren't for me mum, and her box of tricks. What she couldn't do with safety pins was no one's business. Sunday night winkles didn't stand a chance! She'd scurf those little critters from their shells, faster than you could moan, "Gis a jellied eel."

We never had a lot of anything, 'cept pins. They'd turn up in the oddest places, but mainly in your clothes, hems and such. Button off your coat? No problem, she'd pin it shut, from the inside. Everything was from the inside! Don't want the neighbours making snide remarks. So what if you couldn't get the bleedin' fing off again. You stayed warm, melted even, but at least mum saved you from Pneumonia.

Spare street door keys, for when mum had a lunchtime nap. Now that was a favourite. All me mates had key rings. I had a key pin, nappy size. No point wasting the pennies now. Fair enough, but pennies sure didn't help when me bladder was bursting, and the pin jammed in me damn pocket. Fank Gawd we found some string an' started hanging the key behind the letterbox, like everyone else.

Pins were a Godsend, quick fixes, unless of course they were old and bent. They'd catch you unawares then. Ping open and stab you in the sweetshop, or anywhere else for that matter.

P.E lessons were a nightmare sometimes! Me baggy drawers folded at the front and pinned to me vest, from the inside. Leg holes wider than a manhole cover, having whipped out the 'lastic last week to make meself a head band. I queued up for the high jump, Hands by me side, clinging to the scrunched up material like me life depended on it, I took me turn. I went poodling down the hall like a proper lady, trying to keep everyfing intact.

"Use your hands Girl." Miss shouted.

"I am. I am." Suddenly me arms flew up to make the jump. Up an' over that bar, an' somehow managing to land on me knees like a sack of spuds, with drawers gaping and twisted round. Pin still in place but me bum fell out. I felt the stares burning into me, till me cheeks turned crimson. Once me class mates had got over the shock they fell abaht larfing. But d'you know the best thing? Me head band didn't budge a blooming inch.

The Nicker Trilogy

Bare-faced Cheek! 2

"Get yerself over that fish shop now," said Mum, trying to be firm. "Won't take yer long."

"I can't," I moaned for the umpteenth time. "Got no bleedin' drawers on!" Me eyes wide, bulging, trying to get me point across. Me one and only pair were washed an' drying off in front of the gas oven.

"Who's gonna see yer? Yer'll be there an' back before yer know it."

Mum an' me sister Rosie thought it was funny, sending me out to catch me death, exposed to the elements. I could tell by the way they raised their eyebrows an' flicked their heads in that upwards nod fing that everyone did. All right for them, I thought. Ain't no sudden wind gonna whip their skirts up indoors and flash their bits to all an' sundry. I snatched the money off the top of the coal bunker and slammed that street door so hard, it's a wonder the hinges didn't fly off!

"Stroppy mare!" me sister hollered.

I could see the fish shop from the flats. Five minutes an' I'd be back home, warming me toes by the oven. It was no big deal really, but you couldn't just give in to everyfing you were asked to do. You'd never get any peace. So, chips with crackling an' one enormous wally (pickled cucumber) wrapped in newspaper an' tucked under me arm. I saw Mum an' Rosie waving from the balcony, two floors up and closer to heaven than most.

I stepped off the pavement and, fuck me; I got hit by a moped. A bleedin' moped of all fings! The bloke jumped off, shaking like I don't know what. He knelt down beside me, checking out the graze on me knee. "You alright?" he asked.

I just smiled. 'Course I'm bloody well all right! I offen lay down in the road when me muvver's chomping at the bit waiting for her chips.

He scooped me up in his arms. Me skirt blowing abaht all over the shop, an' everyone copping an eyeful. Nine years old an' the pain of embarrassment hurting just as much as the damn draft, whipping me backside to shreds. "Put me down," I said. "Told yer I'm all right. I *can* walk."

Mum an' Rosie ran towards us as we entered the flats. I shut me eyes tight, trying to magic meself somewhere else. The bloke kept apologising to Mum, who could see full well that only me pride had taken a knock. Rosie was relieved that the chip wrapper was still intact. Priorities an' all that!

"We'll take 'er from 'ere," said Mum. But the bloke wasn't listening.

"What floor is it?" he asked. "Second," piped in sis, who started with that upward nod malarkey to mum. It's like an unspoken whisper, drawing yer attention to the bleedin' obvious. Cop a load of this, basically.

Carrying me up them stairs wasn't easy for him. Every time his knee lifted, it was slower than before. Looking over his shoulder I pulled me fiercest face an' mouthed a whopping "Stop it," to me mum an' sister, who were creased up. They had a wicked sense of humour, we all did, but it was always better when someone else was on the receiving end.

Trying to pass off their larfing as a 'worried' reaction, might have fooled the bloke, but not me. Cos I know, if I'd have bin walking behind up those concrete steps, and one of their bums was hanging out like last weeks washing, I'd have wet me bleedin' self!

Now, if he'd have bin an old man with a dodgy leg, he'd have left me in the road, and me worst memory would have bin of a sore knee. But, because he did his best by me, he scarred me mentally for life! Mum an' Rosie too in a round abaht way. 'Cos whenever they mentioned it, an' believe me they did to anyone who stood still long enough, they'd cry real tears an' struggle for breath as they near collapsed in fits of larfter.

—The Nicker Trilogy—

A Roll-on Parlaver. 3

If a boy asked, "will yer go out with me?" it meant he wanted you to be his girlfriend. You got to kiss in the porch of the flats, but mainly you just hung 'round each ovver like best friends.

Martin was me bruvver's friend. He never went out with any girls from the flats. S'pose he was too good for us. He was gorgeous though, with fair hair an' blue eyes, like a film star. Martin was two years older than me.

I remember this particular day very well. I was lacking in drawers, yet again. Gawd knows what happened to 'em. I searched high an' low. Nuffing. Me friends were waiting for me to play out. Rummaging through Rosie's stuff I came across some strange looking drawers. Never seen any fink like 'em before. I dangled 'em in front of her face, as she tried to watch the telly.

"What's these then?" I asked.

"Whatcha fink they are yer dozy cow?

I shrugged me shoulders. "If I knew that I wouldn't be asking."

She flicked 'em away from her face. "They're me 'old yer in drawers, bit like a roll-on."

Well, those roll-on fingy's were abaht eight inches wide and made of the toughest 'lastic ever. Trying to stretch 'em out an' make 'em bigger, pulled all the muscles in your bleedin' arms. Then, soon as you relaxed your grip they'd ping straight back again. Bloody nightmare!

"Whatcha wear these for then?"

"Cos they 'old me belly in don't they."

"Can I borrow 'em? I'm s'posed to be going out with me mates."

Rosie laughed, but gave no answer.

Okay, the roll-on's not rolling anywhere. Arf way up me legs an' its got jammed. I'm pulling, tugging, couldn't even prise me knees apart. Got to move it before it cuts off me circulation. I yanked each side up a fraction at a time. Daren't let go quickly, else it snaps back an' smacks you like a ruler. Getting red in the face and puffing like a chain smoker. Fink I'm gonna die. Arf hour later and, still struggling to breathe, but they're on. Strange though, cos when I tapped me belly it felt an' sounded like week old bread. Fank gawd I'd had a wee beforehand.

I was playing in the area 'round the flats known as the square, when suddenly, the gorgeous Martin called me into the porch by the stairwell. It was dark. Some pillock had nicked the light bulb again. He started kissing me on the mouth. Then, without warning, his hand shot straight up me skirt. I mean, I couldn't feel it on account of the roll-on, but it was up me skirt just the same. "Oi, whatcha fink yer doing?" I asked.

"Nuffing to worry abaht," he said.

How right he was. Not even a tin opener was gonna prise me out of those drawers, fankfully. I could feel him tugging 'round me waist, an' pinching me skin in the process, his face glowing as red as a ripe boil. Five minutes later, an' sounding like he'd just run a relay race, he wheezed. "Whatcha got on 'ere then?"

"It's me roll-on fingy."

"Well what's it s'posed to do ."

"Keep everyfing in," I smiled

"No bloody kidding," he mumbled, and buggered off home to watch the telly. Never came near me again after that...

The Crafty Drag

Dad had a silver coloured baccy tin that lived in his waistcoat pocket. He guarded it like the crown jewels. Scattered on the hearth in the front room lay the remains of his roll-ups, like chopped up sunburnt worms, they were that small! If money was tight dad would sometimes open up these dogends an' add the dried tobacco to the dust in his tin.

Me mates used to buy single ciggies for thrupence each from the newsagents by the school. I used to buy a carrot from the grocers. Everyone smoked. It made you feel grown up! Kids would sneak out of lessons an' hide in the loos for a crafty drag. One day I decided to give it a go.

On the hearth lay the end of one skinny brownish roll-up. I couldn't work out how to light the fing without burning me fingers. With a strip of flaming newspaper Rosie soon had that baccy butt glowing. "Now 'old it between yer finger an' thumb, so that it's pointing towards yer 'and." she said.

So, dogend in place, I put me mouth over the tip of me finger an' sucked in as hard as I could. Me cheeks collapsed inwards. Next fing I knew, the dogend shot straight to the back of me throat an' I swallowed it in one gulp. Nearly killed meself stone dead. Rosie larfed her head off. "Yer're not s'posed to eat the bloody fing." I ran to the scullery for a drink, scared stiff 'case it set light to me belly.

Any money I had would be going on carrots. They lasted longer, an' tasted a site better too!

The Sixties Sweetshop

Sing to the tune of "A few of my favourite things."

Mojo's an' Blackjacks an' pink Flying Saucers
Peardrops, fruit Salads an' Bullseyes in quarters,
Strawberry Bonbons an' Sherbet's galore,
These are the treats that I scrounge pennies for.

Fruit Gums an' Spangles an' square Drumstick lollies
Mallow Bananas an' Merry Maid toffees.
Liquorice Torpedoes. A Chocolate Stick.
Too many Golf Balls have maken me sick!

When Gobstoppers...
chip yer choppers... cos yer've tried to crunch...

A sweet Dummy treat will be softer to eat,
pass Stoppers to friends… to…munch…

Pink Shrimps, Cough Candy's, some Nougat, a Milk Chew.
Honeycomb an' Toffo's, a Kola Kube, now that's new!
Boot an' Shoe Laces, a bleedin' foot long
Victory V's burn yer gob, an' they pong.

Spearmint Pips, Milk Teeth an' some Jelly Babies.
Humbugs an' Love Hearts, Foam Mushrooms are maybes?
Bazooka Joe Bubble Gum, blown in a race,
then some bugger pops it all over yer face!

Aniseed Balls…
Parma Violets… an' a white Choccy Mouse…
I liked to buy old an' new fings to try
an' stuff 'em all in …me …mouth …

Pocket Money

Me an' me sister, Sandy, knocked the neighbours door for old newspapers. Our plan was to make the biggest an' best guy in the area. With trousers an' a shirt taken from the dirty washing cupboard, we laid everyfing out on the bedroom floor, tied the bottom of the trouser legs with string, and set to work.

"Don't scrunch the paper up too small," I said to Sandy, "Else we won't 'ave enough left to stuff the shirt." We cut a circle from a Cornflake packet to make the face. Diving into our big sisters make-up bag, we used pink lipstick for the mouth an' black liquid liner for the eyes. I pinched the torn up newspaper from the lavatory to make the head, an' after a few pokes an' prods our masterpiece was finished. We carried him downstairs in two halves, an' sat him on the pavement outside the flats.

"Penny for the guy, Mister?" We asked, over an' over. We saved people the bother of coming to us, by running to them instead, rattling our tins on the way. No one escaped. Fridays were best for guying. Everyone seemed happier to part with money, when they'd got a wage packet in their pocket. Sometimes anuvver kid would plonk their guy across the road from you. "Oi, we was 'ere first," I'd shout. If they didn't budge it meant running faster to get to the pennies before they did.

With a week to go until bonfire night, Sandy played at her friend Linda's flat 'round the corner. Linda's family were well off, even had their own business! They could easily afford the massive box of fireworks they'd bought for their little girl. The box was emptied onto the carpet an' the girls played 'round with all the brightly coloured packages. No one ever found out how that first firework whizzed abaht the room before setting light to the ovvers. A stray rocket headed straight for the bird cage hanging in the corner. It shot the budgie's legs clean off. The poor fing dropped like a marble onto it's belly and died. The girls ran out into the square. Everfing in the room got ruined. Sandy an Linda weren't allowed to play together again after that. Me sister missed her friend, but I reckon she missed Linda's three wheeled bike, a Gresham Flyer, more? Sandy was offen seen standing in it's boot, being ferried 'round all over the place.

The last two houses on the bombsite had been flattened. Locals started piling up old wood, broken chairs, cupboards, anyfing that would burn. The huge pyramid shape grew bigger by the day. Us kids busied ourselves with the guying, to buy fireworks, or sweets, whichever took our fancy. Everyone gathered 'round on bonfire night. Adults lit the fire an' we'd watch the flames shoot high in the air, the wood hissing an' spitting like unpicked sausages. We kids with our sparklers, bangers, jumping jacks an' warm toasted faces sang at the top of our voices...

> Build a bonfire. Build a bonfire,
> put the teachers on the top,
> stick the prefects in the middle
> an' burn, the bleedin' lot.

We only ever burned our guys of course, 'cept when they were wearing someone's Sunday best.

1965-66 saw the last of the bonfires on that site. The council men cleared the area an' laid large pink slabs ready for the new homes.

Monster cranes blocked the road as the prefabs were hoisted up on fat chains an' swung into place. Two rows, twelve new boxes for families to live in. They had their own little bit of grass at the back, and pots with flowers in at the front. Looked real posh. We soon lost interest though. With Christmas 'round the corner, me an' Sandy made a list of presents we wanted to buy.

While dad was working for Courage's fings weren't too bad. Us young-uns got arf a crown a week each for pocket money. Although this was a small fortune we still needed more to buy the stuff on our list. So, soon as bonfire night was out the way we started with the carol singing.

We'd mostly knock the doors in our own flats. Cos, chances were, if people knew us, they'd be more likely to put their hand in their pocket, an' help to fill our purses. We *never* knocked our friend's doors though! One door that me an' Sandy sung at was opened by an old man. We got through the whole of 'Silent Night' an' best part of 'We Wish You A Merry Christmas' before running out of breathe. Soon as the singing stopped he smiled an' shut the bleedin door. "Oi, Mister," I shouted through the letterbox. "Yer're s'posed to treat us."

"I did," he called back. "I listened to yer, didn't I?"

One night, a week before Christmas, me bruvver Brian shook me awake an' got me out of bed. Easing me arms into a coat, he buttoned me up an' stood back to take a look. Still arf asleep, I could smell the newness of the thick blue fabric with the little grey fur collar. I knew I loved it, even without seeing it properly. A few minutes later I was back in bed an' soon fast asleep.

Mum would buy packs of paper chains. Various coloured strips with gummed backs, that you'd link together. A quick lick on the gummed side, an' you soon had a chain long enough to drape 'round the whole room. Three coloured balloons hanging on cotton an' pinned to the ceiling in each corner. It looked a picture. Even better when Brian came home dragging a Christmas tree behind him.

The excitement of Christmas morning never changed. It didn't matter how little or much yer got, just knowing you had a pillarcase hanging on the end of the bed, made you feel like you would burst with happiness. Nan Filkins would visit beforehand an' bring presents for us. I had the best post office set ever. The stopper on the ink bottle wouldn't twist so I opened it with me teeth, an' had a blue mouth an' tongue for days after.

Nan also carried a tiny tin of magic dust in her handbag, which me an' Sandy would sneak off into the bedroom with. We'd each take a large pinch an' sniff it up our nose, just as we'd seen nan do. If the non-stop sneezing or streaming eyes didn't give us away, then you could guarantee that our snuff coloured moustaches would.

Suddenly, I remembered the coat! I checked the wallrobes incase it had bin hidden away for later. No new coat anywhere in the flat. I guess it didn't fit, an' got sent back.

Kids were good at money making, an' we knew almost every trick in the book. Running errands for the neighbours was easily the favourite, an' somefing you could do all year long. Getting yourself a regular was a bit more difficult, but meant you could make a few bob a week, an' they'd buy yer presents too!

Me an' Sandy happened on anuvver, more daring way. Everyone knew that off licences in pubs paid a penny on all beer an' lemonade bottles returned. It had come to our attention that a first floor flat across the road by the Monkey Park, had loads of the fings lined up like pig's trotters in a butchers window. Our's for the taking. We'd crawl along that landing on all fours, pick up a bottle each, crawl back to the stairs an' pop it in a carrier bag. A few trips back an' forth an' we'd earned ourselves a tanner each, plus a coatin from mum when she saw the state of our bleedin' knees!

We were never gonna be rich, but some days I reckon we had more money in our pockets than a lot of the adults!

Favourite TV Programmes.

Twizzle, (puppet) 1957 0nwards
Torchey, the little battery boy (puppet) 1959-1960
Sara & Hoppity (puppets) 1962-1963
Fireball XL5 (puppets) Space adventure 1962
Opportunity Knocks. Talent Show. 1956-1977
The Five O/Clock Club, (similar to Blue Peter) 1963-1966
The Avengers. Crime busters. 1961-1969
Bonanza. Western. 1959 onwards.
Emergency Ward 10. Medical drama. 1957-1967
Peyton Place. The first soap! 1964-1969
77 Sunset Strip. Private Investigators. Up to 1964.
The fugitive. 1963-1967
The Lucy Show. Comedy. 1962-1968
Ready Steady Go. Music Showcase. 1963-1966
Petticoat Junction. Western Comedy. 1963-1970
Lost in Space. Space travel Family. 1965-1969
Skippy the Kangaroo. 1967
Rin Tin Tin. Boy and Dog rescuers. 1954-1959
Rawhide. Cowboy. 1959-1966
Mystery and Imagination. Spooky Stories. 1966-1970
Beverley Hillbillies. 1960s onwards.
Z Cars. Merseyside Police Drama. 1962
Batman. 1966-1968
Till Death Us Do Part. Comedy. 1966-1974
Sunday Night at the London Palladium. Variety Acts. Up to 1967

Check out the early 'puppet' programmes on U Tube.

—Culinary Delights—

We were pretty hard up some of the time, an' brassic for the rest of it. Eight kids to feed an' hardly any money coming in. Although the food cupboard was offen empty, we'd have school dinners to fall back on, so we didn't do so bad. Mum shopped daily, just buying in what we needed, or what she could afford. Some days were good an' we'd eat like Lawds, not very offen but they did happen. Then there were the hungry days, when no amount of moaning would ease the ache in yer belly.

We were called some names in our time, but skinny wasn't one of 'em. 'Cept in mum's case. Finn as a rake, an' could get blown away by a breeze, according to Nan.

Sometimes, we'd have a Sunday evening fishy treat! 'Sing Something Simple' playing on the wireless. Mum buzzing round in her wrap-over paisley pinny. Her hair lost beneath the turban style head scarf, which was tied up on the top with the ends tucked in, leaving one 'Dinky' curler poking out the front. The open fire roaring into life after dad held the mat against it to 'draw' the fing, the scorched underside smelling stronger than his baccy.

Dad would then pull the table out to the middle of the room. Us four young-uns would dive on the chairs an' try to be first to grab the safety pin. All the while trying not to wake the baby, sleeping in her lemon wicker crib by the fire.

Whelks, cockles an' winkles night, with a quart of shrimps thrown in for good measure. Once you'd scurfed those winkles from their shells with the pin, you'd drown 'em in vinegar an' help 'em on their way with a slice of bread. "'andsome," Dad would say. I liked to drink the vinegar afterwards but Mum said not to. "It'll dry up yer blood." So I only sneaked a mouthful if her back was turned, else she'd go off alarming.

All this, washed down with a cup of tea. Tea was secondary to breathing, an' the kettle always on a low gas. If the meter ran out an' you hadn't got a shilling you could stick the kettle on the fire, or pop a piece of cardboard in the meter. Tea was a fixer, (bit like safety pins). If you were bored, scared, worried, sick, or just couldn't fink straight, a cup of Brooke Bond Dividened would sort you out. Dad liked to sup his from a saucer.

Some food stuffs that I liked had me friends turning their noses up. They'd never even tried fings like a fried egg sandwich! Bread an' dripping, with it's beef flavoured veins an' spread arf inch fick, or Cornflakes, doused in hot water with a dash of sterilized milk. Whoever heard of putting cows milk on flakes anyway? Wasn't normal.

One of me favourite 'tide you over' examples, was Buppy Milk.

Ingredients:

Slice of white bread.

Arf a cup of milk.

Spoon of sugar.

Break bread into pieces and put in bowl. Cover with hot milk. Sprinkle on sugar.

Sometimes hard to eat. Cos bread becomes soft an' sloppyfied an' slips off the damn spoon. But otherwise, very nice.

Mum was a good cook, when the pennies allowed. Stew with pearl barley was like heaven in a pot, and if she added dumplings, well, you just dribbled like a baby. Couldn't help yerself. Apple dumpling, although rare, was another favourite. Big as a football, well almost! Wrapped in a pudding cloth and left to bubble away for hours. Once cooked, it was gone in minutes, nothing remaining ovver than it's warm sweet scent filling every room of the flat.

Our neighbour old Lil was a good cook too, according to Mum. She lived upstairs on the fourth floor, friend of me mum an' the local butcher. He would bung her a bit extra, try an' build her up. Lil was like a little doll, an' married to old Bill who was enormous. Lil looked out for me mum an' would cook her up special treats. She'd come downstairs with her Pyrex bowl covered with a tea towel, an' find mum in the scullery. "'Ere yer go girl," she'd say. "Get that down yerself." Mum's face lit up like her whole world was in that dish, only sweeter tasting.

She loved tripe an' onions, sometimes called convalescence food. Can't fink why? 'Nough to make yer bloody sick in the first place, but mum loved the stuff. White pieces of cows stomach lining floating abaht in milk, flavoured with onion. Just the ticket! I'd watch as bit by bit she popped it into her mouth. I imagined it snaking its slimy way past her tonsil's an' into her own stomach, unaided. Didn't need chewing, which was just as well, cos her bottom set of false teeth had bin lost for ages. I fink Sandy chucked 'em down the rubbish chute?

Dad wasn't really a betting man, but he did like a flutter on the Derby. His favourite jockey, Scobie Breasley, was riding Santa Claus in 1964. Emptying his pockets onto the betting office counter, he placed his bet. Mum an' dad came home in a good mood. They were so happy an' smiley that it had us kids worried. It wasn't the usual carry-on! Dad's horse had won. The food cupboard that week was filled to bursting, never seen anyfing like it in me life! We just didn't know what to eat first.

The boy who lived downstairs tried to show me up once in front of his mates. "Your family eats shit," he larfed. I didn't know if he meant we had rubbish food, or that we were just horrible. We weren't a model family, we knew that. An' it's true we didn't have much, but we still had each ovver, especially us young-uns, an' that had to count for somefing. We stood each ovvers corner, offen.

I wanted to say somefing clever but the words didn't happen. So I did the next best fing, I waited for him 'round the corner an' found the courage to give him a 'nuckle sandwich instead, then ran for me life. That soon shut the bastard up, and it didn't cost me a penny neither!

─To see or not to see─

Mum said it only wanders when I'm tired! In which case I must have bin arf asleep most of the time, cos some of the kids at school noticed. I felt upset when remarks were made, but rarely let on. Now an' then I'd stick up for meself an' answer back, like the day in the dinner hall, tucking into me jam roly poly. The boy sitting opposite kept staring, like I'd got a bogey on me nose or somefing. "Where's yer goggles then," he piped up, trying to impress his friend.

"Mind yer own business."

"Why's yer eyeball doing that?"

"Doing what?" I asked.

"Sitting in the corner."

"It's 'aving a bleedin' rest. Whatcha fink its fuckin' doing?"

Me proper mates 'round the flats never mentioned me wonky eye, s'pect that's cos they were me mates an' it didn't matter to 'em. 'Sides, I weren't the only one! There were a few kids abaht with eyes that wandered off, somefing to do with catching measles as a baby. Me an' Alfie both had the measles.

Mr Law, at Guys Hospital tried to help us, with his box of lenses an' wall charts. I never wanted much, just to be special like a beautiful princess, with ribbons, long lacy frocks an' normal eyes. Mr Law handed me an' Alfie our glasses, blue for boys an' pink for girls.

Mine had a white plaster stuck over one of the lenses. "It will help to make your eye stronger," he promised. None of the princesses I'd seen on the telly wore goggles. I hated 'em. They were ugly an' I couldn't see right.

A week later, Alfie an' meself stood on the landing of the flats. "Bet I can throw mine further than yor's," he boasted.

With glasses in hand, we counted to three an' lobbed those fings over that balcony so hard; we nearly yanked our arms from their sockets. Whizzing' through the air like rockets; they ended up smashed to smithereens in the swing park below, and guess who won? The girl with the eyeball that stared round corner's of course, little me.

Trick

Lick nails of the two forefingers. Stick on 2 x small bits
of paper. Sing song. Fly away Peter = take hand over back of shoulder, prise off paper with base of thumb and bring back. Repeat for Paul. Come back Peter = back over the shoulder and try to attached paper again, bring hand forward. Repeat for Paul.

Two little dickey birds sitting on a wall
One named Peter one named Paul
Fly away Peter fly away Paul
Come back Peter come back Paul.

—Nitty Nora—

School medicals were good for one fing, they got you out of some of the boring lessons. The first time I was given a brown envelope I was chuffed to bits, an' smiled so big that it made me face ache. I'd won a prize, or so I'd thought. Me mate nudged me in the ribs. Her mouth turned down at the corners. "What's that for then?" she asked. "Why ain't I got one?" I shrugged me shoulders. "Well I don't know, do I. Ask 'em." I felt really special, which of course I was. I HAD NITS! 'Cept I didn't know it at the time.

Mum detested letters in brown envelopes. They made her nervous. "What's it say?" I asked. She never answered. Taking the scissors from the sideboard drawer, she cut me hair off. Straight 'round in a line below me ears. I stamped me feet an' bawled like a baby. Made no difference, she carried on, only now the line was wonkier.

Mum sent me to the chemist with a note, an' afterwards plastered me head with the slimy yellow nit lotion, 'Suleo'. It smelt horrible an' made me hair stiff. Cried me eyes out, again. "I'll wash it off tomorrow," said Mum. "Now go out an' play, there's a good girl." I stood there sulking. "I want me 'air back, now."

Mum looked upset. She explained that short hair was easier to keep clean. "It'll grow back in no time," she promised.

I went downstairs an' played in the porch, happily chalking on the wall. Me friends came out. They were okay, never took any notice of me hair. Then some new kids came into the block, started pointing an' larfing, holding their nose an' calling me names. I scooted up those stairs faster than the rent man on pay days.

Mum dried me soggy face, tied a scarf round me head an' sent me off again, looking like a little granny. All Parents told their kids the same fing. "Sticks an' stones may break yer bones but names will never 'urt yer." They bleedin' well lied. Names did hurt, an' sometimes even more-so than a kick up the bum.

Next time I got a brown envelope I gave it to me mate.

Sometimes, me an' Sandy were sent to a clinic off the Borough Road. The Nitty Norah there was old an' thin. Her face all crinkled like screwed up rag. She wore little round glasses that perched near the tip of her nose, an' she hated kids. Once Norah got you in that chair you were done for. No escaping. Didn't matter how much pain she caused, if you dared to pull away she'd scurf you straight back again, with a warning. "Don't you come that nonsense with me my girl." She tugged your hair this way an' that, an' dragged that metal comb backwards across your scalp till your skin burned. Convinced that our head's now had more holes than a tea strainer, an' was spurting blood like a mini fountain, we cried.

 Dad said she didn't know how to treat kids. He called her an old spinster. Me an' Sandy called her a fucking old cow.

─Dressing Up─

When Yvonne an' her Gran moved into the flats from some foreign country, telling tales of thieves having their hands chopped off an' people being eaten by crocodiles, I was glad I lived in Walworth. Yvonne was eighteen, a bit old to be me friend, but I didn't mind, I still liked her. She taught me a tune on the piano that took up a whole wall in their front room, an' she wore her ginger hair in a bun, just like a teacher. Me bruvver Brian fancied her rotten. He would offen say to me, "Give 'er a message. Tell 'er this …" An' I'd say, "tell 'er yer bleedin' self."

Brian would lug bags of coal from the lorry and hump 'em up the stairs for his customers, an' still have breath left to wolf-whistle Yvonne! She didn't fall for his charms, he wasn't her type. Strange that, as most people loved him, 'specially the girls. Normally they couldn't resist his cheeky, smiley ways, an' would fall over 'emselves for a chance to be his bird. I remember two girls having a barny in the square, ending up with lots of slapping an' hair pulling. Me sister Rosie had to step in an' break 'em up. I was secretly pleased Yvonne didn't fancy him, after all, she was *my* friend. I found her first.

I fink she dealt in secondhand stuff, cos now an' then she'd leave a sack of old clothes outside our door. Most of 'em were no good to anyone, but we'd still keep 'em for when the rag an' bone man did his rounds. Sometimes he'd give a couple of bob for a bundle, but mostly he'd hand over a goldfish swimming abaht in a see through plastic bag. "What's the good of that?" Dad would joke. "Ardly worth the bother of putting me teeth in for."

This particular day there were two frocks in the sack that I fell in love with. The first, a white lacy bride one, had me prancing abaht the square showing everyone how glamorous I looked. "Whatcha wearing that fing for?" Asked me mate.

"I'm gonna marry Colin."

"Does he know abaht it?"

"No, 'aven't told 'im yet, but 'e will when 'e sees me all dressed up." Colin refused to come out an' play. He called out from behind his street door. "I don't want to see yer, an' I don't want to get married neither."

The second, a bright red frock for a big lady, had multi coloured parrots all over it. I lopped the bottom off to make meself a skirt an' top. With needle an' thread I sat on the stairs of the landing, stitching away. Old Bill, from the fourth floor came an' sat beside me. He taught me a back stitch to make the seams stronger. I whipped the 'lastic from me sister's drawers, an' with the help of mum's hairclip, I forced it through the waistband. A ten year old dressmaker in the family, mum was chuffed. The top fell apart within a week, but I wore that skirt for months!

I hardly saw Yvonne once she got herself a boyfriend. She spent a lot of time too with her beatnik mates over the West End. She took me big sister Rosie there one night to meet 'em all. Dressed in black an' white, with big earrings and dark eye make-up, Rosie looked really different. Her backcombed hair kept in place with a good few squirts of sugar water, mum's alternative for the 'no lacquer' days. It would take a month of Sundays to comb out!

A few days later a beatnik boy came knocking at our flat. Mum opened the door, an' when she saw his long black coat, almost trailing the floor, she nearly passed out! She thought he was an undertaker. He never came back again.

Yvonne saved me from harm once, though I never got to tell her. I'd bin to the shop for me mum. Soon as I reached the first landing a bloke jumped out from behind the balcony wall. He stared kissing me all over the face an' neck. I stood there like a nitwit, too scared to do or say anyfing. Yvonne an' her new boyfriend were smooching further up the stairs. Soon as they started talking the bloke disappeared. Running into the flat I told me bruvvers. Brian, Charlie an' Terry all dashed out after him. We were both lucky that day, me, cos of Yvonne, an' the bloke for managing to hide. Cos, if me bruvvers had caught him, he'd have bin pushing up daisies in two seconds flat!

I missed Yvonne, but still had me ovver friends, an' lots of stuff to be finking abaht. I'm glad Colin didn't want to get married as I had new plans now. I wanted to be on the telly like Sharon from school. I nearly choked on me biscuit when I saw her pop up in the telly adverts, tapping away on the new Petite Typewriter. She gave me the phone number of the agency in New Bond Street. The lady at the dry cleaners, who I helped out sometimes, let me use her phone to make the appointment. All I had to do now was tell me mum an' find something nice to wear.

By strange coincidence, a neighbour 'round the block gave me a new mint green frock and a white petticoat. They were the nicest fings you ever saw, an' fitted like they were made 'specially for me.

Me an' mum walked into the busy office, bigger than our front room! Between us we filled in the details on the form, and waited. Two hours later an' still waiting…

I overheard a staff lady telling anuvver, "Strip her down to her underwear, and I'll be with you in a few minutes."

"Did yer 'ear that?" I whispered to mum.

She nodded. "Don't worry, that'll be for the older girls, like the ones in the catalogues."

I wasn't convinced. I felt scared an' fidgety. I'd bin sat there for two hours waiting to show off me new frock. I wasn't abaht to be stripped off an' have some stranger gawping at me drawers. 'Sides, in me panic I couldn't even remember if they were arf decent or not. Knowing *my* luck they were probably held up with a pin.

The woman behind the desk was busy fiddling with her nails, scraping the ends with a bright pink lolly stick. "Can't we just say that we 'ave to go?" I suggested to mum. A few minutes later we were back at the bus stop. Never really wanted to be in adverts anyway.

We stopped off for pie mash down Westmorland Road. I chatted away between forkfuls of mash an' spoonfuls of liquor. Poor mum couldn't get a word in edgeways. "Did I tell yer I'm going on Opportunity Knocks Mum? I've already written to get an audition…

—Unspoken.—

Aunt Ann, mum's favourite sister, had a smiley, happy face an' a mop of dark curly hair. She was blind, deaf, larfed a lot and grew mint in the back garden by the roses. She was married to Bill, a bit of a fatso who worked close to home as an odd-job man an' decorator. Every weekday lunchtime, in paint splattered overalls he'd eat cheese an' pickle sandwiches in Aunt Ann's warm an' tidy kitchen. Uncle Bill was a child molester.

Whenever school broke up, either me or Sandy would travel by buses to Southend, to stay with them for a week or more. Sometimes we'd go together, which was always more fun. We looked on it as a holiday, a chance to go somewhere different an' meet with the friends we'd made, in an' 'round the streets. There weren't any flats to block out the sunshine, just rows an' rows of houses with pretty front gardens an' white painted fences. "The fresh air will do yer the world of good," Mum would say. "Yer'll sleep like babies." Me an' Sandy just smiled, but never said a word. We knew different.

Up the road from Aunt Ann's was a grassed area with houses set 'round it. Me an' Sandy would roller skate there for hours. Sometimes we'd grab the pushbikes from the shed, an' belt 'round that green as fast as we could, larfing an' effing an' blinding abaht our growing skills. Thought we were the bee's knees, especially since we didn't have bikes at home. The neighbours would tell us off abaht our language. We'd listen but wouldn't take much notice. Swearing was part of who we were, never meant any harm. They didn't swear in Southend, at least we never heard 'em.

Some days I'd feel all grown-up when taking Aunt Ann to the shops. She'd have a white stick in one hand an' be hanging onto me arm with the ovver. Clipped on the top of her dress sat her hearing aid box. When this was switched on she heard everyfing I said, 'cept of course when it started its bleedin' whistling racket, then no one could hear anyfing anyway. Aunt Ann would stop an' chat to friends several times along the way. She knew everyone, an' everyone loved her. I'd offen keep shifting me weight from one foot to the ovver, like a silent 'hello,' I'm still here. Hoping she'd talk faster, or make excuses to get going. She never did.

I offen wondered what it must be like inside her head. She wasn't always blind. Doctors at the Hospital tried to save the sight in her bad eye, an' ended up damaging both of 'em. She was abaht thirty when it all went black. It never stopped her doing fings though. She cooked lovely dinners, knitted jumpers, made strange rugs, an' she put the decorations up at Christmas, even stood on tables to push pins in the ceiling.

Uncle Bill helped by doing housework. He started to nag Aunt Ann abaht the state of the front room furniture. "The settee and chairs have seen better days," he said, "Time we had some different ones." Anyone could see they still looked like new. Anyone 'cept me aunt that is. Soon afterwards, the furniture disappeared and in its place stood a tatty old secondhand suite, that me own mum wouldn't have given houseroom to, not even if it came gift-wrapped!

Uncle Bill's ovver job was to look after the garden, his pride an' joy. 'It had the cleanest dirt ever! No weed dared to raise its head in *those* borders. Sometimes I'd watch him picking up stray leaves or lopping off flowers before they fell an' made a mess on the grass. He offen had a strange smile, like he was sickly or somefing. He was a lot smarter than us kids. We always tried to outwit him, but he had an answer for everyfing. There were four fings he had to keep reminding me abaht.

I'm not to lock me bedroom door at bedtime, incase there's a fire.

I mustn't wear underwear in bed, cos a body needs to breathe.

I have to let him in the bathroom to wash me back.

I'm not to pick the fruit in the garden.

No wonder he went nuts when me an' Sandy kicked a football at his little apple tree, snapping off one of the branches. We broke his deckchair that day too, both making a dive for it at the same time. Me little finger got crushed flat by the wooden frame an' hurt like mad. I should have bin bawling me eyes out, but we fell abaht larfing instead. The more he told us to pack it in the more we larfed, just couldn't help ourselves. He wasn't happy.

Uncle Bill usually worked in the houses on the other side of town, through a park that had cattle grids by each gate so the animals couldn't escape. Fink they must have already scarpered, cos I'd never seen any. He would ride his pushbike along the dirt path, sometimes with me perched on the crossbar. Having decorated the house of a woman over there, they became friends an' he would offen drop by for somefing or ovver. She had five children. One day Sandy was taken on a visit there, an' she told me that her eyes nearly popped out her head. There in the front room was Aunt Ann's lovely three piece suite.

When me an' Sandy were in Southend together we felt stronger an' fings were more bearable. She tried to tell Aunt Ann abaht what was going on. "You're a wicked wicked girl for saying such things. I'll be telling your uncle when he comes home for lunch. Sandy was scared. She needn't have bin though, cos Aunt Ann must have forgotten all abaht it. It was never mentioned again.

When we were there separately we were quiet, well behaved an' wouldn't say boo to a goose. I liked Southend. It seemed bigger an' brighter than London, an' a lot cleaner. There was more open space with trees an' fings. The roads looked wider an' the pavements were offen empty (always good for skating). I hated being there on me own though.

Daytimes were mostly okay while Uncle Bill was out at work, but evening times were different, everyfing changed. After dinner we'd sit in the front room. Me aunt all cosy in the stinky rotten old armchair, knitting needles clicking away. She'd switch off her hearing aids to block the sound from the telly. Don't know if she realised, but she always had a little smile on her face. She must have bin happy in her life.

Me an' Uncle Bill sat on the settee. He'd put his hand between me legs an' start doing stuff. Sometimes he'd be reading a newspaper with one hand an' touching me up with the ovver. Aunt Ann's needles still tap-tapping. If I reached over I could have touched her, we were that close! When bedtime came, snuggled beneath the covers I'd screw me eyes tight shut, trying to get to sleep as fast as possible, an' stay that way till morning. It never made any difference. I was always woken during the night to find him under the blanket examining me by torchlight. Never knew what to do abaht it, so just pretended I was still sleeping, it seemed the best fing to do.

We went to the local funfair once, in the town. Me uncle held me hand all the way there. He warned me abaht talking to strangers, men in particular. "Never go off with anyone," he said. "Some men aren't nice. They'll do bad things to you."

It was soon after me eleventh birthday that I stopped going to Southend. Don't know how or why it came abaht, it just did, an' I never questioned it. I was safer at home. It wasn't so easy for Sandy though. Uncle Bill had taken a real shine to her. They would even come to the flat an' take her away on holiday with 'em. "Give your mum a break," he'd say. Poor Sandy, I felt really sorry for her. We still never said anyfing though. No one would have believed us anyway.

Whenever I smell mint in a garden I always fink of Aunt Ann an' smile.

If ever I see white, paint splattered overalls, the little girl hidden deep inside me, remembers Uncle Bill, an' cries.

Playtime

Mums an' Dads didn't play much with their kids. They'd sit in the park with you or treat you to a day at the seaside, but never did any of the running abaht stuff. You had to get out there an' make yer own fun.

Spud guns, marbles, conkers, skipping games an' home made catapults were just some of the fings we enjoyed. We'd hold Secret Seven club meetings in an empty pram shed, kitted out with orange boxes for seats an' candles to see what we were finking abaht.

Balancing along the finn top edge of railings, like tight-rope walkers, was slow an' risky. 'Specially if you were a bit of a short arse like me, it seemed a long way to fall. We'd have competitions to see which of us made it the furthest. There wouldn't be any prizes, but not spraining our ankles or breaking our necks when we lost balance an' fell off, was reward enough for anyone.

Keeping an eye out for old mattresses was somefing we all did. Occasionally one would get lobbed out of a bedroom window for the council men to take away. 'Cept we'd grab it first, an' drag it 'round to the grassed area. Scrambling up the wall onto the roof of the garages, we'd run like the clappers an' fly off the end like ten ton birds with 'nackered wings. Fingers crossed an' praying that some joker hadn't nipped round an' whipped the mattress out of position.

Running games like IT an' Tin Tan Tommy were regular favourites. One of the games us girls liked best was Kiss Chase. The boys offen kicked up a fuss abaht playing this, but always gave in. An' you didn't have to be a brain box to notice 'em making 'emselves catchable targets neither.

Playground Song

Yer own choice of boys or girls name.

I love you Jimmy, oh yes I do.
I love you Jimmy, it's true.
When you're not near me, I'm blue.
Oh Jimmy, I love you.

Street Games

Knock Down Ginger.

This was a favourite. Could play this one by yourself if you were bored. Just knock someone's door an' run off an' hide. Watch as they curse and holler cos you've dragged them out of their chair for nuffing. Give them time to sit down again, and have another go!

Another option.

Tie a long length of string to the knocker, get yourself out of sight an' yank away to your hearts content. But get ready to run! Some just untie the string, but ovvers follow it back and catch you red-handed.

Tin Tan Tommy.

For this you'd need an empty tin, bean size, an' some friends. If you're Tommy it's yer job to guard the tin. Friends run off an' hide, but never too far away. You walk round trying to spot them. If you see someone you have to get back and bash the tin on the ground, an' shout Tin Tan Tommy. Then that friend's out of the game. If they get to the tin before you, then you're out. Everyone comes back to the tin, ready to run off an' start all over again. Simple!

Cannon.

You need five strips of wood, abaht eight inches long. Lean four bits against the wall, a couple of inches apart. The fifth piece balances along the top, like a wicket. You also need some friends and a ball, tennis size. If you're the bowler, standing a few feet back you aim the ball at the wicket. Soon as the sticks fall you friends scatter but stay in sight. They have to try an' get back to re-build the wicket. Only one friend at a time mind! You can only stop them by throwing and hitting them with the ball. Then they're out. If you miss and they build the wicket, they become the bowler.

Normally, one friend gets to place only one stick, since the idea is to dodge the ball and get away, giving someone else a chance. If you get to put the fifth stick on top, then you're the winner.

The bowler gets three chances to knock the wicket down. If he misses someone else has a turn.

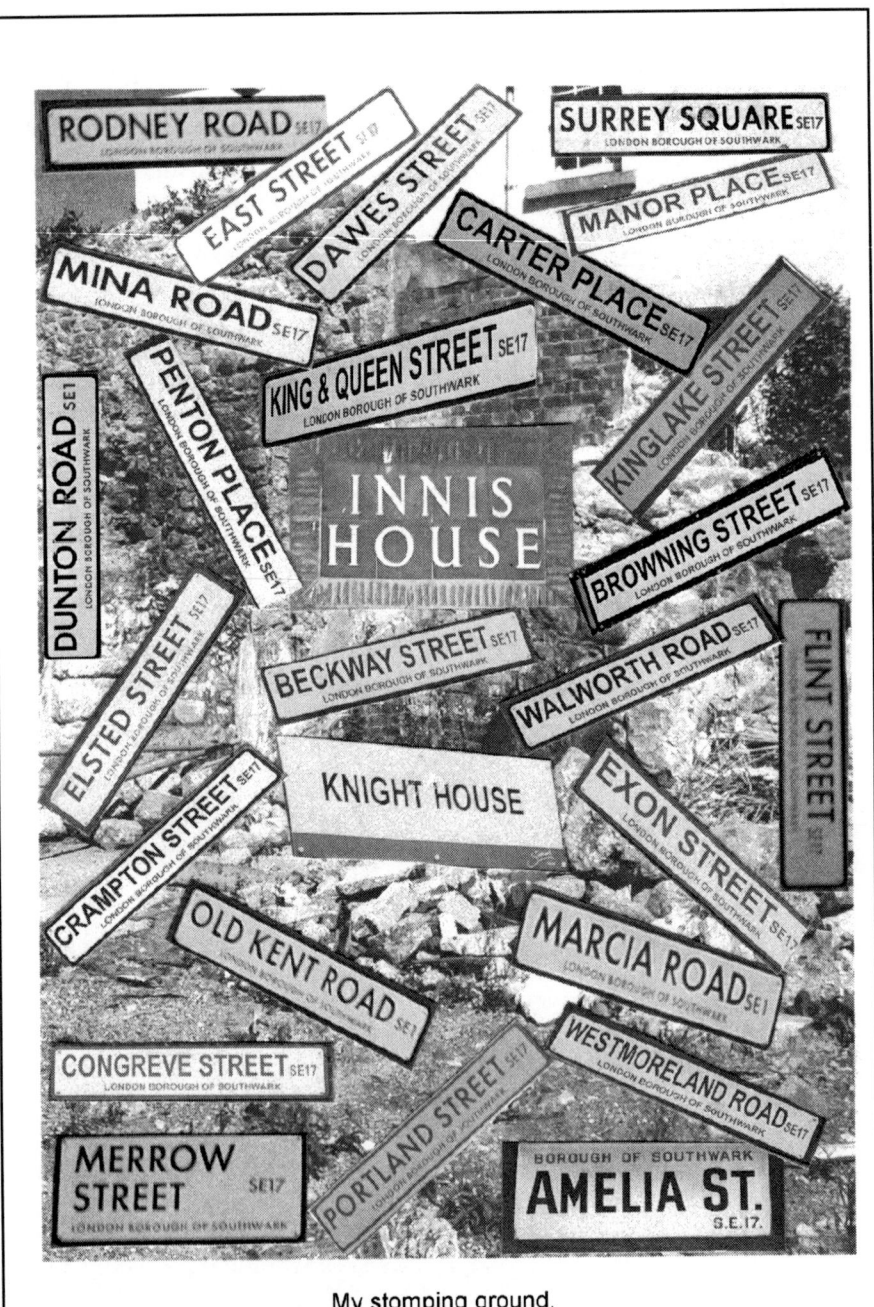

My stomping ground.

The Thomas A Beckett Pub where the famous boxers trained.
Photo courtesy of Southwark Local History Library.

The clock with the 'lifting bowler', above Carters Men's & Boys Outfitters. Old Kent Road.
Photo courtesy of Southwark Local History Library.

East Street Market (known as The Lane) early 1960s
Picture Courtesy of southwark local History Library.

1. LONDON LIFE: Costermonger "Pearly Kings and Queens" in Southwark. *Photo: G.P.U.*

Photo courtesy of Southwark Local History Library.

Original 1960s Pramsheds

1960s Memorabilia

83

—Wheels—

Me an' me sister Sandy were skate mad! We'd spend hours buzzing 'round the streets. I remember the first time we struggled to put 'em on, clomping 'round like would be ballet dancers in army boots, arms an' legs all over the place. We spent more time on our knees an' bums, than upright, but still bounced back for anuvver go. We didn't have fancy leather straps like some, ours were held in place with mum's old stockings, wound round an' round for the tightest fit. They never came loose no matter how hard we worked 'em.

In no time at all we were as good as some an' better than ovvers, tearing abaht, dodging people, prams an' homemade carts. At breakneck speed we'd bomb along the pavements trying to race the cars. The only way to stop our wheels (greased up with marg) was to crash into railings or a lamp post. We never mastered an easier option, 'cept maybe to do a quick turn, but chances were we'd trip over our own feet an' end up face down kissing the concrete, losing arf our nose in the process. Railings were best, they never bit back!

We travelled miles 'round Walworth, sometimes I'd hold onto a length of string tied to the back of a boys bike. "Faster, faster," I'd yell. The speed an' vibration of the wheels made yer feet tingle like pins an' needles. The boy would never call out when he'd had enough. He would either stop dead without warning an' you'd slam into the back of him, or he'd fly round a corner, leaving you praying for a lamp post ahead, a neighbour, anyfing that wouldn't hurt too much!

Skating was somefing girls did, bit like skipping. Boys preferred their bikes or handmade carts, made up of pram wheels, a plank of wood, an orange box for a seat an' a length of string to steer with. Carts had no breaking system either. Racing our bruvver Alfie in his was easy peasey. With the ground being so flat he needed a friend to push from behind, till he built up enough speed. By which time the friend had buggered off an' left him to it.

Our greased up skate wheels had a life of their own. Me an' Sandy would stand larfing our socks off at the finishing post. "Get a bleeding' move on. Be dark soon," we'd tease. Alfie tugged his steering string to turn those front wheels an' make the fing stop. The sudden change in direction would flip the cart over an' chuck him out. He never got hurt. "Tough as old boots is Alfie," I'd heard me Dad say.

Dragging the cart behind, he'd head back to the flats hoping to spy a mate on the way who fancied a muck abaht with the wheels. It seemed that boys spent more time pulling carts than riding on 'em. Pulling was one fing, but getting 'em going with a mate sat in an orange box on top was too much like hard work.

Didn't matter how strong the boys tried to make 'em, carts never seemed to last long. They were usually battered, buckled an' broken by the end of the day, an' dumped in the chute with all the ovver rubbish.

Our skates went on forever though. A twist with a spanner an' the size was adjusted to fit our growing feet. Finding a pair of mum's old stockings to use as straps wasn't always as easy, an' a couple of times we just had to make do with her best pair! For which she always fanked us.

Skipping an' Ball games

Playing two balls (tennis size) against the wall was one of the more skilful games. All sorts of actions would come into play, offen dictated by your choice of song. Your turn would continue till you made a mistake or dropped the ball by accident. The kids who were really clever made fings even harder for 'emselves. They'd go through the same song over an' over, adding a different level of skill each time. Like, playing one-handed or blindsey, (eyes closed). Dropsy, (allowing the ball to bounce off the floor between each throw), or even clapsey, (clapping each time a ball left yer hand). There were lots of tricks included, too many to mention. A game could easily last an hour or more. Here is my favourite ball game song.

> Over the garden wall
> I let me baby fall.
> Me muvver came out an' gave me a clout
> I asked her what it was all abaht.
> She gave me anuvver to match the ovver.
> Over the garden wall.

Every girl had a Skipping Rope. If it wasn't a shop bought one, then you made do with a length of plastic coated washing line, which we preferred anyway. It turned much faster and made a loud whooshing sound, 'specially when you did the bumps, (allowing the rope to circle twice with one jump). Gawd help your poor legs if you misjudged fings. That washing line would bite into your skin an' leave a welt type mark for most of the day. As with the ball songs, you would carry out all the actions in the skipping ones too.

Skipping Songs.

Up an' down. Up an' down
all the way to London town.
Swish swash swish swash
all the way to Charing Cross.
Leg swing leg swing
all the way to Berlin.
Heel toe heel toe
all the way to Mexico.
Legs apart legs apart
all the way to Hyde Park.

*

Shorter version.

Up an down
Swish swash
Leg swing
Heel toe
Legs apart.
One.
*

Lead skipper jumps in and sings following song.

"I like coffee I like tea, I like (friends name) in with me."
Friend jumps in an' both skip together. Lead skipper sings
"Don't like coffee don't like tea, don't like (friends name) in with me."
Friend jumps out. Lead skipper gets to choose someone else.

First Love

I met Billy Boyle when I was eleven. He started hanging 'round our flats with his mates. They would ride like maniacs through the square on their bikes, showing off as usual. Till one of the bigger ones, a boy named Freddie came a cropper. Hitting a kerb at the wrong angle, he lay sprawled on the concrete. Didn't look arf as clever nursing a fat ankle. "Oi, whatcha fink yer looking at?" he spat. I stared him out, unblinking, just like me bruvver Alfie taught me. "Nuffing much," I answered. He snarled like the giant poodle that lived 'round the corner, but he didn't scare me. Billy, his best mate, leant against the railings in front of the grassed area, an' smiled across at me. That was all it took! I loved him from that moment on.

Couldn't wait to tell me sister Rosie all abaht him. How he looked like Paul McCartney from the Beatles, with one little difference, the hair colour. Billy's was a dark orange, bit like rust, but it really suited him. I mentioned his trousers too, an' how his knees shone through the frayed and gaping holes. "Yeah, alright, give it a rest," she grinned, then started teasing till me cheeks burned red as radishes.

After school hours I played 'round the square, offen missing me favourite telly just incase he came by. Billy lived with his dad in the flats along Kinglake Street, abaht five minutes away. There was never any mention of a mum. Could be she ran off with the Milkman. Women did that. I heard me own mum say so.

Saturday morning I'd arranged to meet me new mate Gina down East Lane Market. She was staying at her nan's for a few months, to give her mum a break. With her nan living in the old houses down the end of Blendon Row, Gina only had to fall out of bed an' she was smack, bang, in the middle of the stalls, well almost, lucky cow. Maybe lucky's not quite right, since Blendon had more rats than people. They scooted across her bed during the night, an' every morning she checked that her toes hadn't bin nibbled off!

"Where yer bin?" I moaned, standing beneath a stalls canopy, trying to dodge the drizzle. The piece of cardboard tucked in me shoe to cover the little hole, was soaked through an' letting the water in."'Ad to run an errand for me Granddad," she said. "D'yer get that frock yet?" she asked. "No, bin waiting abaht for you." The stalls had their regular pitches so we knew exactly where to head for.

I'd bin running errands for all the neighbours the passed two weeks, no wonder me bleedin' shoes were falling apart. But it had all bin worth it. There in front of me hung the prettiest little shift frock in the world. Its pink paisley pattern an' long front zip, with the large silver ring pull, just happened to be the latest fing, an' soon to be all mine! "There yer go darling." smiled the stall holder. I counted out the money into his hand, thirty bob an' not a penny more.

Sandie Shaw's record, 'Long Live Love' played loud through the many transistors. Dripping like me baby sister's nose, I stood an' listened to every word. This would be me an' Billy's song, forever. "D'yer wanna come 'round tonight?" asked Gina. "Me nan an' granddad will be in the pub. Billy can come too, if yer like."

"Ok," I said, an' ran off home. Couldn't wait to try me new frock on.

I never saw Gina very much. She went to a different school. During the summer holidays all schools would open as play centres with lots of fun fings going on. That's how we met. A line of kids swaggering up an' down the hall doing the Lambeth Walk. Thumbs curled under make believe trouser braces, music blaring an' us all singing our hearts out. Me an' Gina, in line one behind the ovver, were busy watching Buster, a boy from Dunton Bridge, acting the goat. Not realising the dance had finished, we crashed into each ovver an' ended up on our bums. Some People said we looked similar with our short brown hair an' round faces, bit like sisters.

Me bruvver Alfie walked me back down the Lane to Blendon. The stalls had packed up an' gone. Council workers cleared away the rubbish an' boxes left on the kerbside. It was back to being an ordinary street again.

Gina's nan an' granddad had already left, so we piled records on the radiogram an' threw ourselves abaht like the dancers on 'Top of the Pops', until Billy started banging at the door. I became shy Maggie again. I really wanted him to like me, an' me new frock which he didn't seem to notice! Having changed the records over, I couldn't believe me eyes when I turned 'round. They were sitting there on the settee, kissing! Didn't know what to do or say, so crept out the front door an' ran all the way home. Could feel me heart pounding as I imagined allsorts of horrors jumping out of the shadows. I wouldn't stop though, not till I was safe indoors.

It wasn't fair. Billy was nearly *my* boyfriend an' I wanted to kiss him, but couldn't. I'd bin practising on the back of me hand like most girls did. At least I'd know what to do when it happened for real. Boys always liked Gina better than me. She was mouthier, funnier, an' a bit of a dare-devil, an' for tuppence she'd show 'em her fanny.

With me twelfth birthday only a week away, Rosie offered to do a birthday tea. I'd never had one before, I was so excited. "Can I invite Billy?" I asked. "Course yer can. Invite whoever yer want, only not too many," she smiled. Rosie did really good. She made jelly an' sandwiches an' bought fairy cakes an' lemonade from her own wages.

The table was laid up all proper like. Dusty Springfield was singing away on the wireless an', wearing me zipper frock, I waited.

Rosie jumped up. "I'll get the door," she said. Billy came into the front room as she called me into the scullery. "Who else is coming?" she asked.

"No one."

"What? Yer didn't invite anyone else?"

"No. It's *my* tea. Yer said I could ask as many as I liked."

"So, what 'appened?"

"Nuffing. I only asked one."

Me sister shook her head an' larfed, then came an' helped us eat the sandwiches.

Later that evening me an' Billy hung 'round downstairs in the porch. From out of the blue he wrapped his arms 'round me waist, so I draped mine 'round his neck an' linked me hand's together. Once we'd sorted out how to get closer without breaking noses, his mouth found mine. Our lips puckered up an' sealed like sink plungers. We became statues. I closed me eyes like the actors did on the telly, 'cept every few seconds I'd take a sneaky peek through one eye to check if Billy was doing the same. We never knew how long a kiss was s'posed to last, so just stood there, waiting for somefing to happen.

Rosie's boyfriend Tony had seen us from the road an' came running over. "That's not 'ow yer do it," he said, sticking his hands on the back of our heads an' jiggling us abaht a bit. "Need to get some movement going," he instructed. So suddenly I felt like Noddy, me head was all over the place but me mouth stayed in the same position. Didn't feel anyfing really, 'cept arms ache.

If being Billy's girlfriend, (even though he still hadn't asked me out yet) meant kissing, then I was happy to practise some more on the back of me hand. I loved him that much!

—Milton House—

Sandy crouched down behind the bushes lining the main road. Her little head popping up every few seconds as she waited for a bus, any bus that would take her home. She hadn't planned on making a run for it; it happened purely by chance.

The Hospitals isolation rooms were divided by large glass panels. Sandy would knock on the window an' talk with the old lady next door. At nine years old an' barely tall enough for her chin to rest on the wooden ledge, she opened her heart to the lady with custard coloured skin. "They took me away from me sister. Maggie's still locked up," she said. "I wanna go 'ome. Don't like being on me own," she cried.

With the nursing staff busy sorting lunches, Sandy was called into the next room by way of a bent an' beckoning finger. The yellow lady gave her ten bob an' a beaming smile.

No one seemed to notice the little girl on the bus wearing patterned pyjamas an' pink felt slippers. The conductor gave her numbers of the three buses needed in order to reach the Old Kent Road. Eventually she made it to the flats an' hid on the stairs to the third landing. Hearing someone dump rubbish down the chute she poked her head 'round the corner. "Dad," she called in a loud whisper. Dad's eyes, bright as pearly buttons, as he took those stairs two at a time to reach his girl. He hugged her tight before sneaking her into a neighbours flat for safety.

Shut inside an empty larder, Sandy peeped through the holes in the air vent. She watched as the policemen went in to search our flat, an' smiled to herself when they came out empty-handed. Soon as the coast was clear, she crept along the landing an' into our flat. Mum kept shaking her head. She had a hard time believing that her little girl had managed to find her way home. "Well I did," said Sandy, feeling all grown up an' wolfing down anuvver of her favourite Lincoln biscuits. By teatime, our bruvver Brian took her to Carter Street Police Station cos it was the right fing to do. She was back in the Hospital that same evening.

The yellow lady looked surprised to see her again so soon. Sandy couldn't wait to tell her what went on. "I got to see me Mum an' Dad," she grinned. Leaning closer, she lowered her voice. "The police kept on abaht the money, but I never told 'em where I got it from. 'Onest."

First I knew of it was when I got summoned to the Matrons office. Mrs Davis was a big lady with a miserable face. I stood in front of her desk trying me hardest to fink of what I'd done wrong!

"Your sister has run away from the Hospital. Do you know anything about this?" she asked.

I shook me head. "No, nuffing."

"Where is she likely to go?"

Stupid question, I thought. Where would any scared nine year old head for. I shrugged me shoulders. "No idea," I said, an' was dismissed back to the school room.

Being sent to a remand centre came as a shock to everyone. Me an' Sandy had bin to court before for 'hopping the wag,' but had always bin allowed home again with a warning. This time was different. We stood in front of the Judge, with Mum an' Rosie alongside us. "Tell me why you don't go to school?" the Judge asked. I glanced abaht, expecting the answer to drop out of finn air. It didn't. Sandy nudged me to say somefing quick. "We've bin sick," I blurted.

"What's been the problem?"

"Don't know. Just 'aven't bin well," was the best I could offer.

The Judge spoke quietly to those 'round her before turning her attention back to us. "Under the circumstances you will be placed on remand for two weeks," she said, "for medical reports."

Me an' Sandy stared at each ovver in shock, couldn't believe our ears, she must have got it wrong? No one sends kids away for hopping the wag! Mums legs buckled an' she fainted backwards onto a chair. A woman officer dashed across to help. Rosie burst out crying, wrapping her arms tightly 'round the both of us. "Yer can't lock 'em up, they're just kids." she shouted over an' over, but the officers weren't really listening, which was just as well, cos I was scared that she'd get locked up too! Me an' Sandy were led away downstairs to the holding room, to wait for transport.

There were already six girls in the dark green van with its barred windows. Me an' Sandy sat together. No one spoke. A girl sitting alone on the back seat, face pressed into an enormous teddy, sobbed quietly throughout the journey. I couldn't help but wonder what she'd bin up to, but never got to find out.

First stop was Cumberlow Lodge. The girls were ordered off, leaving just me an' Sandy behind. Minutes later the engine started up an' we were on our way again. A road sign ahead read Croydon, which, although I'd never bin there before, I knew wasn't a million miles from home. Soon after, we pulled up in front of a large house on a busy road. A girl's face peered down from an upstairs window.

After meeting the head, Mrs Davis, we were taken down to the basement by a staff member. The stairs were steep an' narrow, an' led to a darkish room with one tiny barred window looking out on the garden. There were toilet cubicles, washing machines an' big tin cupboards stacked with piles of neatly folded clothes, in colours of grey an' green. The staff member, Mrs B, whose name I just couldn't get me tongue 'round, chose outfits for us, then led us back upstairs to the communal bathroom.

Having filled the baths, she stood there staring while we took off our clothes. Feeling shy an' embarrassed I fumbled nervously with the hook on me new first bra, white with red rosebuds, given me by me bruvver Brian's girlfriend. Mrs B sneered an' chucked it to the floor. "Don't know why you're wearing that thing," she said. "You've got nothing to put in it." After our baths she yanked a comb across our heads searching for nits. She was a scary cow an' I hated her already.

There were eight girls at Milton House all sitting 'round chatting in the main room. Me an' Sandy sat down an' hardly spoke a word to anyone. Later that night, tucked in me bed, I couldn't stop finking abaht the Doctors visit planned for the morning, an' the report he was s'posed to write. No matter how many faces we'd practised pulling, we just didn't look sick! He'd know for sure we'd bin swinging the lead.

Our family Doctor at home had bin easy to fool. He offen wrote me out a certificate to stay off school. I'd put on a painful, strangled type voice, give a few coughs an' told him I was just too ill, an' that was that. Fank gawd mum didn't have to come to the appointments with me.

"It'll be okay," I told Sandy, as we waited to be called into the medical room, fingers crossed tight behind me back. The man in the dark suit took gadgets from his black case an' laid 'em on the table. He never said much, but wrote lots. I passed all his checks with flying colours, but Sandy had a rash on her back so they carted her off to the Hospital. She'd only bin there a couple of days when she did a runner.

I shared a room with two girls, Lyn aged twelve same as me, an' Gill aged sixteen. Daytimes at Milton House were not too bad; there were lots of fings to keep you busy, like the dreaded school lessons. We also had to set the tables for meals an' clear away afterwards. We even got to go to Church on Sundays, once we'd shown we could be trusted. Night times weren't so good. I couldn't sleep for worrying abaht me sister, an' finking of mum an' dad an' how much I missed 'em. Although there were ovver kids' abaht, sometimes I'd cry into me pillar cos I felt lonely. Mrs Green, one of the helpers, would sit by me bed just talking an' trying to cheer me up. She was lovely an' kind an' smelt of peppermint. I liked her a lot.

At the beginning of the second week I got summoned to the office again. I *knew* I hadn't done anyfing wrong, so weren't abaht to give meself gutsache over it. Maybe Sandy had done anuvver bunk? I saw Mrs Davis smile for the first time. "Your sister is ready to leave the Hospital. Would you like to go with the staff to pick her up?" I was that excited I almost wanted to give her a cuddle.

Me an' Sandy threw our arms 'round each ovver, smiling away as we walked to the car. I really missed her. I had no trouble getting to sleep after that. Me sister was safe in the next room, an' that's all that mattered. In a few days we'd be home an' everyfing would be back to normal.

One afternoon meself an' room-mate Lyn went to the basement to put some clothes away. Hearing voices out the back we peered through the tiny open window. With our faces pressed against the bars we called to the workmen close by, sunning 'emselves on a tea break an' smoking like troupers. "Got a spare fag, Mister," we asked.

After some persuading they handed over a lighted ciggie. Me an' Lyn puffed an' coughed, went dizzy in the head and coughed again. The door to the basement creaked open. Mrs B shouted from the top of the stairs. "Haven't you girls finished yet?"

"Just done Miss," we hollered back, praying for all our worth that she didn't smell the smoke. Gawd knows what would have happened, didn't bear finking abaht. We decided it best not to take chances again, until Carol, from the front bedroom came up with a great idea. "Let's climb out the window tonight an' run away." It didn't seem to matter that we were on the first floor with no means of climbing down the wall! We were little kids with big ideas. It gave us somefing else to fink abaht ovver than maths, English lessons and court dates. After our baths, an' with each item of clothing counted by the staff, we crept back to the bedroom to plan our escape. Within minutes the rain started running down the window in drunken lines. "But we 'aven't got any coats," said one girl. "We'll get soaked through an' stiff with the cold," she added in her best drama queen voice. We all nodded. She had a point. We didn't have to go that particular night. We snuggled down in our cosy beds instead. Maybe we'll escape tomorrow, if it's warmer?

The remand home wasn't the worst place in the world. They treated us well so long as we behaved. All the while there were fings going on you could almost forget that you were locked up. But during the quiet times, when family an' friends all crowded back in your head, it was only then that you realised what you were missing out on.

The night before court Lyn an' meself were jumping abaht on the beds. Gill was having a strop an' nagging us to pack it in, else end up in trouble. Not sure what happened but we pulled the curtains off the rail. Plastic hooks flying everywhere! "Yer've gone an' done it now," said Gill, in a fed up mumsey tone. She stuck her head under the covers an' left us to it. Mum's curtains at home were threaded on wires. I didn't know how the hook fingy's worked so couldn't fix 'em properly. Somehow we managed to hang the curtains back.

Mrs B started her usual morning rounds, by bursting into the room with a high pitched " Get out of those beds now." Going across to the window, in one swift movement she threw the curtains wide, they flew off the rail an' ended up in a heap on the floor. Poor Gill got a right telling off. Being the eldest she should have had more control over us young ones, like it was her place to keep us in check. I did whisper 'sorry' before me an' Sandy got back on the van though. "Better late than never," me Mum always told me.

Dad stood waiting at the entrance to the court. It was so good to see him; I could have hugged him forever. Our names were called an' once again we were led into the court room. Fings weren't looking too clever. Boarding school kept cropping up, like it had already bin decided on. Dad pleaded our case, an' like the hero he was, got to take us home, for good. We promised him an' ourselves that we'd never end up in one of those places again. We had a probation officer breathing down our necks for two years, just to make sure we kept our word.

Playground Rhyme

What's the time?
Arf passed nine
'ang yer 'nickers on the line.
If a Copper comes along,
'urry up an put 'em on.

—Night Raiders—

Its not like we needed the stupid bed in the first place. The hop-picking hut had barely room to house us four kids, let alone some fold up contraption, that the ole girl several huts along, wanted rid of.

"Yer never know when it might come in 'andy," said Mum. She said the same abaht me dad too, in one of her jokey moments. Anyway, us kids slept two up three down in a double feather bed, that sagged in the middle like homemade sponge. It was cosy, warm and safe. The only fing likely to scare the life out of you was a late night ghost story … Oh yeah, and un-cut toenails.

I fink the invasion started the night I caught a nasty niff. I elbowed me sister and told her, "Get over yer own side." I was sure she'd blown off again. She clouted me one and rolled away. It smelt like distemper, the stuff dad painted the walls with. Gawd knows why it was on me pillar.

We soon realised that this was their calling card. If you whiffed that distemper stuff, it meant they were close by your face, if not already on it. Either way you were under attack, an' the last fing you needed was a bug in your lughole. So we thrashed about in that bed like no ones business. Squashing and splatting, taking no prisoners.

Bed Bugs were flat and round and reddish brown. greedy little critters. They'd suck you dry, well almost, then bugger off to sleep in some dark cubby hole 'till their next feed. Sometimes we'd see 'em during the day, sneaking behind a poster of Billy Fury, in readiness for the nightly onslaught.

They couldn't jump or fly, but cor blimey were they smart! They'd crawl up the wall and free-fall onto the bed, like kamikaze dive bombers. An' before you were any the wiser, they'd pierce you with their tubes, first one, then the ovver.

Bet you didn't know that? Well, neither did I then, but I made it my business to find out, incase I happened on 'em in the future. Super glue at the ready, I'll jam their little pipe works.

First, they inject you with their saliva. No ordinary dribble this, it comes loaded with ammo! anesthetics an' anticoagulants. Bit of a mouthful on any day of the week. An' for anyone who hasn't come across the anti word before, it means …

"THEY- THIN -YOUR- BLOOD,"

on account of making it easier to suck through the second tube.

So, now they got you all comfortable an' numbed up, they go in for the kill, supping that crimson juice till their bellies are fit to pop. Poor mum, she was beside herself. Strange expression that, never did understand what it meant, don't fink she did neither. Anyway, that's where she was, an' embarrassed too, like it was her fault that we were contaminated.

People shared more back then. Nuffing got wasted. Anyfing with a bit of life left in it, old dog, whatever, soon got snapped up. There was a stigma attached to some fings though, like head lice. You didn't breathe a word. None of your mates ever asked why your hair was plastered in gunk. Didn't have to, they'd had their turn the week before.

After six weeks of the nightly assaults, the hop-picking season ended an' we headed home, taking only the clothes on our backs. Couldn't chance any stowaways looking for a free ride.

Two things I've learnt as a result. There are many myths surrounding these little vampires, and most of 'em are a load of old codswallop. Their requirements are minimal. Firstly, you need to be breathing, since they want their fix of carbon dioxide. Secondly, they like their prey warm. So, all in all, if you're not dead then you're a target, regardless.

The moral of this story being, beware of strangers bearing gifts. You may get more than you bargained for. Because …

"THEY ARE STILL OUT THERE!"

Hop-picking

Stilsted Farm

"There were five in the bed an' the little one said, roll over, roll over. So we all rolled over an' bleedin' bedlam. Us kids ended up in a play fight, arms an' legs everywhere. Larfing and screaming like you've never heard, till Mum came in an' put a stop to it."Yer'll wake the dead in a minute. Keep the noise down, d'yer 'ear me?"

These brick huts weren't our usual ones. They had no beds, just a double mattress on the floor, leaving room enough at your feet to dump your clothes, either on the wooden chair or the floor. It was our own fault though as we turned up late. All the best ones got snapped up early. We were still lucky mind, an' better off than those who arrived at the very last minute. They had no choice but to sleep in the corrugated tin ones down the end of the farm. Ovens, we called 'em. Mum said you could get sunstroke without even stepping outside.

Our usual two huts had loads of furniture an' stuff that people left behind over the years. A double bed in one, an' a table an' couple of armchairs in the ovver, a a mirror, some pictures an' crockery too. Even had two little mats! Not much room for anyfing else. There were no windows an' no electrics. Oil lamps hung from hooks on the walls, or we used candles stuck on saucers.

Hop-picking was the best fun ever! Our yearly holiday, even though it meant getting up soon after you'd gone asleep, least that's how it felt. Mum never had to wake us, the farm boy on the tractor did that. Each morning abaht six o/clock he'd dump four faggots outside each hut, (large bundles of twigs for the cookhouse fire). Mum would sneak out and get the fire going. The large charred kettle, filled from one of the standpipes dotted abaht the farm, hung over the flames, for the first smoke flavoured tea of the day.

Every morning was the same. Soon as you'd opened that hut door the smell of damp burning wood drifted up your nose. Streams of grey smoke creeping out of all the little chimneys. A real country smell, mum called it. We loved it. Next, you needed your wellies on, cos the grass was always soaked with dew an' alive with creepy crawlies.

The shower an' toilet blocks were next to each ovver in the middle of the farm. Us girls never used the showers. Everyone knew that the boys spied on you through the holes they'd made in the walls. Dirty sods. So, after our tea we'd wash from a bowl in the huts. Then have breakfast, mainly bread, speared on forks an' toasted in front of the fire.

The pickers started early. The more you picked the more money you made. Mum was a good picker, her fingers stripped those hops from their stems faster than a waving hand. She'd bin going to the farms since she was a teenager. She helped her own parents in the forties. Then when she married dad they would go to the Beltring Farm in Paddock Wood. I'd never bin to that one.

It was a long walk to the hop field, made your legs feel like they was gonna drop off. Most people took sandwiches an' stayed all day, saved traipsing back an' forth. A few nipped off at lunchtime to start preparing the dinner, saving time later.

The hop bin itself was a huge canvas bag on a fick wooden frame. Either side stood a tall pole with four bines on. You'd yank a bine down an' chuck it across the bin, and start picking off those hops as quick as you could. Once those bines were done the bin would be moved down to the next poles, an' so on. At midday an' evening time the measurer would come along with his basket. Each basketful (known as a bushel) would earn mum abaht 2/-6d. All these amounts were written in his book an' the monies paid out by the Farmer at the end of the season, unless of course you pestered him for subs, in which case you usually ended up going home with next to nuffing. But that was okay too, cos everyone had a good time along the way.

Us kids weren't much help to mum, although we picked, we seemed to spend more time running off an' getting up to no good. We'd play in the corn fields, or climb up the haystacks. Pick blackberries from the hedgerows or roll abaht on an old mattress dumped in a ditch. Sometimes, we'd paddle in the stream that ran through the farm, fishing for tiddlers in jam jars tied with string. Scrumping was somefing else that most people did. We'd fill our buckets an' nag mum to turn 'em into apple dumpling. Wrapped in a cloth the large ball of dough would bubble away in the black cauldron, (mum's hopping pot) over the cookhouse fire.

It was this year that Rosie got to grips with her first snake! She'd told some boy who was sweet on her, that she wasn't interested. He came by the hut next day clutching a cornflake packet. As Rosie turned away, he emptied the grass snake from the packet down the back of her dress. What a racket! She screamed an' hollered an' called him some choice names. Then she punched his face in. Rosie was good at looking after herself. He didn't mess with her again.

Hops ponged like cheesy feet an' dirty socks, an' turned your fingers green. After awhile that green became black an' sticky, an' was a bugger to get off. It didn't matter though cos we were all stained the same.

The sun always seemed to shine over the hop farm. We were never jealous of our friends who spent their holidays at the seaside, cos we had more than our fair share of fun. Most people had a transistor propped up by their bin, an' we'd all sing along to our favourite songs. It was such a happy time.

One afternoon me an' mum walked the long winding lane to the Farmer's house. Mum stayed out of sight alongside a bush. "Just give 'im the note an' wait for the money." We offen had to ask for a sub. "Don't let 'im know I'm 'ere. Are yer listening to me?"

The Farmer was described as a nice friendly sort by the grown-ups. We'd offen see him strolling 'round the farm, in mud caked wellies, chatting away to the hoppers. He scared me little sister Mary, witless. Never knew why, but she screamed blue murder whenever she clapped eyes on him.

Handing me an envelope for mum, he said, "I'm going back that way, let me give you a lift." Could hardly say no, but felt really bad. Poor mum would have to walk back all on her own. As we turned the first bend, there she was in full view, I pretended I hadn't noticed. "Isn't that your Mum?" He asked.

"Where?" I said, trying to sound surprised. "No, never seen 'er before in me life."

He smiled an' carried on driving. Fink I fooled him.

There were hardly any strangers among the pickers. Most were regulars an' came from the same area of London. They travelled down using any means they could. Some by train an' ovvers by van or small open backed lorries, like *we* did once. Well exciting.

On Saturday evenings people dressed smarter. Wellies an' headscarfs left in the huts. The men would organise a massive bonfire. Everyone gathered 'round. Beer cans an' bottles in carrier bags an' boxes, with lemonade an' crisps for the kids. Taters dotted abaht the fires edge. Crumpets an' bread toasting on forks or long thin sticks. The roaring fire, spitting and crackling away in the darkness, shooting sparks high into the air, gave the whole evening a feeling of magic, like you could burst any minute with excitement. Some mums an' kids larfing an' dancing along to the blaring music, all wireless' tuned to the same station. Song of the season in 66 was 'Little Man' by Sonny an' Cher. We all knew the words to that one. We were one big happy family, having the time of our life.

Mum's sister an' family came to visit one Friday night. Dad came too, for the weekend. We all spent the evening at the village pub, the only one for miles! Making our way back along the never ending lane in the dark, was a bit of a nightmare. With only one torch between us we managed to dodge most of the brambles and ditches. Someone suggested a short cut, so we piled through the opening in the hedge, an' ended up in some overgrown field. The noise of the crickets and ovver small creatures darting here an' there gave us kids the creeps. We were glad to be back in the cookhouse.

"Where's Dad?" asked Alfie. Everyone glanced 'round at the same time. Mum looked over towards the main gate, "E'll be back in a minute, don't worry." Dad turned up soon after. We just stared as he moved closer to the cookhouse fire. No one said a word. He was dripping from head to toe in some bad smelling gunk. A giggle escaped from one of us kids. "What 'appened to you then?" asked Mum, "Where've yer bin?"

Dad wiped his hanky across his forehead. "Didn't yer 'ear me calling yer, girl?" he said.

"Calling? Whatcha talking abaht?" said Mum, looking over at us kids. We shrugged our shoulders.

"In a bloody swamp, that's where I've bin. No fanks to you lot."

"Well I didn't know, did I. Thought yer were behind us."

"I was," said Dad. Who wandered off to the shower block to sort himself out. Us kids did larf abaht it, but only cos he looked such a site, an' didn't smell too good. Felt really sorry for him though, poor fing. It must have bin really scary. Bet he couldn't wait to get back on that train for home.

The final day of the season arrived, along with the Farmer, his pocket book an' wages for the hoppers. Everyone busy packing up their belongings, an' saying their goodbyes. It was always a sad time, none of us kids ever wanted to leave. Mum double checked that nuffing had been overlooked. We left, knowing only one fing for sure, we'd be back again same time next year.

Playground Rhyme

Lulu had a baby
she called it Sonny Jim
she took it to the swimming baths
to see if it could swim
it swan to the bottom
it swan to the top
Lulu got excited
an' grabbed it by it's
Cockles
seven pence a glass
an' If you don't like 'em
shove 'em up your
ask no questions tell no lies
ever see a copper doing up his
flies are a nuisance
bugs are worst
this is the end of my very silly verse.

East Lane Market

"Come on ladies don't be shy now. Serve yer ole mans dinner up on this beauty an' e'll treat yer like a Duchess. Money back if 'e don't, 'less of course the poor sods short-sighted." This regular stallholder had the gift of the gab an' no mistake. He'd balance a large serving dish on his arm, an' throw plates, bowls, cup and saucers onto it, all set out in a pretty pattern. Then, he'd chuck the whole lot across to his helper without breaking a single fing!

The crowd couldn't get enough. Mum reckoned he must stay up most nights practising. Women pushed forward waving their money, scared to miss out on the bargain. He had 'em eating out of his hand. Those who didn't have money to throw away on new crockery, would hang 'round anyway just to watch the show, an' listen to his banter. He was a young, cheeky, flirty character, and they loved him to bits. You couldn't help but stand an' watch.

East Lane Market was a bit of a circus at the weekends, filled with everyfing you'd ever need in all shapes, sizes an' colours. Apart from the endless rails of clothes, the jewels (shilling a necklace), flowers an' fruit, there was steaming hot glasses of sarsaparilla on the cold winter mornings. Cockles an' jellied eels were lined up on little saucers an' the smell of roasting chestnuts had people flocking if only to warm their frozen fingers an' faces.

It was a great place to spend your time, an' you needed time too. It would be packed. Everyone taking pigeon steps. People pushing an' shoving an' ankles being chewed by the loaded bags an' pushchairs.

Toes flattened by the bleedin' clodhoppers who couldn't care less where they stepped. You had no choice but to go with the crowd. Sometimes, nervous looking 'fly boys' would park 'emselves on a corner an' flog their dodgy gear from a suitcase. Everyone wanted a bargain.

The shopkeepers in the lane brought lots of their goods outside onto the pavements, leaving even less space for us to move abaht in.

Sold me dad's petrol lighter there when he was broke. It matched his baccy tin, but it had to go. Had a little pack of flints an' a petrol refill fingy too, which looked an' felt like a squidgy little bomb, bit like a bottle teat. I stood outside the café, tapping men on the arm. "Wanna buy a lighter Mister?" Too shy to do that shouting out malarkey. Dad wanted five bob but I only managed to get arf a crown. Still, he was happy with that.

I always made a point of getting to the end of the market first, by the Walworth Road. The man there sold puppies an' kittens from a box, a fiver each. I'd stroke an' pet 'em every week, always wanting to buy 'em all. Terry, one of me bruvvers brought a rabbit home once. Mum went spare and shut it in the bathroom. She had a brown plastic shopping bag stuck under the sink, the rabbit chewed through one side and came out the ovver. Mum was fuming. The rabbit disappeared soon after that.

The Lane cafes were always full. Most people mainly popping in for a warm, an' to give their feet a rest. A mug of tea, a smoke, an' a chat then off again, while ovvers would stick around for the fried breakfast with a dollop of bubble an' squeak on the side. The smoke in these places was like a blue, grey fog, hanging 'round like a low ceiling. Never bothered anyone. All cafes an' pubs were the same.

Just 'round the back of the Lane in Dawes Street was 'Jacks', the second-hand dealer. His stalls were in what I can only describe as a massive wooden shed. He sold mainly clothes, these were piled a foot high. Anyfing an' everyfink all jumbled up together. Women nudged each other out the way to get a closer look. Mum liked sorting through all that stuff. Jack had a shop too, on a corner down Rodney Road. This was mainly filled with bits of furniture an' old toys. He had a sewing machine there once, an' I wanted it *so* bad, I kept on at me mum for ages. She would have bought it for me too, if we'd had the money to spare.

Oh, I nearly forgot abaht the monkey! You could get your photo taken down the Lane holding a little monkey in a suit. It's tiny face was as sweet as a sherbet dib-dab. Me little sister an' Terry had theirs done. I reckon the man made a fortune, cos people were always queuing. It was somefing different. After all, most of us had never seen one before, 'cept on the telly. I was eleven when I saw me first real chicken with a head! an' I had to go to Kent for that.

Everyone loved the Lane. I heard that Charlie Chaplin was born down there somewhere? Don't know abaht that, but he did live in Browning Street when he was two, an' that's official.

A Pub Crawl

Everyone loved the weekends. For the mum's an' dad's it meant putting on the glad rags an' having a good time in the pub. Gawd knows there were enough to choose from. Most had jukeboxes for weekday evenings, but weekends were different, they were special. The landlord would book someone to play the piano. Everyone sang along to the old tunes. Some women would hitch their skirts up, mum too, for a bit of 'knee's up' dancing.

> "Knees up Muvverr Brown. Knees up Muvver Brown.
> Under the table you must go
> ee-i-ee-i-ee-i-oh
> If I catch yer bending, I'll saw yer legs right off.
> Knees up knees up, don't get the breeze up.
> Knees up Muvver Brown.

Sometimes people would take turns singing on the little stage. Everyone clapped, cheered an' smiled, lots of larfing an' happy faces, always. The seafood man with his tray of cockles an' whelks, hanging from a strap 'round his neck, weaved in an' out the tables, an' offen sold out within the hour.

People worked all week to pay for their weekend's fun, or so it seemed. When there weren't enough money to settle their bills, somehow they'd find the few bob needed for a round, even if it meant borrowing from a neighbour.

For some of us kids there were times when we had to drag along. We'd sit on the step outside the public bar of The Castle, in Old Kent Road. A glass of orange squash balanced on our knee, if we were lucky. I'd poke me head round the door, search out mum's face through the sea of bodies and call, "Are yer nearly ready yet?" She would call back in a loud whisper, "Shut the door yer causing a draft. I won't be a minute." Mum's minutes went on forever!

It was boring on the step an' you had to keep ducking out the way to let people in an' out, else get trod on. The concrete dipped in the middle from all the bums that had bin plonked there. Mum said it wasn't good to sit on damp concrete or grass, but pub doorsteps didn't seem to count. If you were crafty enough you could hide just inside the door behind the heavy velvet curtain.

Next door to the 'Castle', on the corner of Marcia Road was Carter's, a men's outfitters. A real posh shop where the staff had stern faces an' tape measures hanging round their neck. Above the shop front was an enormous clock, with a man's dummy head stuck on top of it, wearing a bowler hat. Dad told me that when the clock struck the hour the bowler hat lifted up. I watched that bleedin clock, lots! I never saw that hat move once. Dad bought a flat cap from Carter's once, but nuffing else mind. "Yer'd have to rob a bank to afford those prices," people said.

Me Mum an' Dad liked their Guinness. "It's good for your blood," the Doctor told 'em. Must have tasted rotten though, cos it took 'em bleedin' ages to drink the stuff. One of their friends drank gin. She was always snivelling abaht somefing or ovver. Mum told me that some people ain't happy 'less they're miserable an' eye lotion, as she called it, makes you like that.

Up the road a bit was the Dun Cow, anuvver family pub which had a little stage too. Me bruvver Brian used to go in there with his mate an' sing their favourite Al Jolson songs.

Pubs usually had two bars, a public one for the working class, and a saloon bar for so-called posher people, where the piano lived. Come Saturday evenings everyone crowed into the saloon, eager to add their voices to the sings songs. Sometimes there would be a snug. This was offen much smaller an' seemed to be where the really old girls would sit.

Mum an' Dad hardly ever used the Dun Cow or the Thomas A Beckett, a bit further along on the corner of Albany Road. Older people normally stuck to their locals, where they knew everyone an' didn't have far to stagger home when the bell sounded.

The Thomas A Beckett was known by everyone. Even us kids knew that famous boxers trained in the upstairs gym, don't remember seeing any though. Fans would come from all over the country to that pub. Henry Cooper, Joe Frazier and Muhammed Ali all trained there. Dad did some boxing in his younger days, so I was told. I'd like to fink that he had bin to that gym, sparred in that ring with some famous names, or at least rubbed shoulders with 'em.

Most people from our flats used the two smaller locals, the Bedford Arms on the corner of Beckway Street, or the Hen 'n' Chicks in Alvey Street, opposite Surrey Square. The doorstep of this pub wasn't a bad place to be, since Bills, the sweetshop next door sold Jubblies (frozen orange squash in a triangular carton). These would keep any grizzling nipper quiet, forever!

I will always remember the Hen 'n' Chicks for giving me one of me best memories. I was abaht seven years old. With Christmas coming up the Landlord organised a trip for his customer's children. I'd never seen a show before, 'cept on the telly. I was excited an' scared all at the same time an' didn't know what to expect. Joe Brown an' his Bruvvers sang on the stage an' later Mr Pastry came on, spilling flour everywhere, falling abaht an' acting silly. We larfed till our bellies hurt an' shouted our heads off. It was the best time ever. I didn't want it to end.

Two pubs that we heard a lot abaht from the 'boys' were the Charlie Chaplin at the Elephant an' Castle an' a new one called the Apples an' Pears, off the Old Kent road. These places were for young people, no sing-songs going on there! Just loud pop music an' regular surprise visits from the Old Bill. Me bruvvers were handcuffed once just for their lip and got chucked in the back of a 'Black Mariah' an' carted off to Tower Bridge nick, where they got to spend the night.

Drunks were funny, from a distance, either really happy or as miserable as sin, an' wanting to fight the world. One fing for sure though, they couldn't run for toffee! Sometimes me an' Sandy watched from the safety of the balcony. A lone drunk, swaying an' cursing his way back to his poor family, pissed as a newt, an' falling against the pram sheds. We'd larf when he ended up on his bum an' shouted stuff that sounded like baby nonsense.

Some did scary stuff too! Like the time Charley, me bruvver, nearly killed us all in our beds. I woke in the middle of the night, while everyone else was still busy snoring their heads off.

A strong, rotten smell filled the whole room. I yanked the blanket over me head to block me nose off, an' stop me feeling sick, but It didn't work. Creeping from the bed I went out to the scullery. Charley sat slumped over the cooker with all the gases on. I couldn't move him on me own so rushed to get mum. Sneaking in the rooms we opened all the windows to let the gas out. It was bloody freezing.

Charley slept in the chair till morning. Don't fink he remembered, cos he never ever mentioned it.

For most kids, mum an' dad in the pub at the weekend was as normal as milk in your tea. It's just the way fings were. They met with their friends an' neighbours, forgot their troubles for a few hours, an' were geared up to face the ups an' downs waiting 'round the corner.

Sometimes though, I'd find me mum, or me dad, sitting in a pub on their own, no one else in the bar, no one to talk to. Just taking in the pattern on the red, 'fuzzy feeling' wallpaper, just passing the time …

─Hard Up Options─

The Pawnshop

I didn't care abaht me bruvvers stuff, but I did care abaht me mum. If she got found out gawd know's what would happen?

She pushed the bedroom door shut and opened the walldrobe. "Don't breathe a word of this, d'yer 'ear." Mum whispered.

"But 'e'll find out," I said. "Then we'll really be in for it."

Mum folded the sports jacket and black trousers before placing them in the carrier bag. "They'll be back before he misses 'em. You mark my words" she smiled.

The boys bedroom was always tidy, nuffing out of place. Charlie, the eldest, was very particular. His shelf in the walldrobe was laid out regimental style. You daren't breathe for fear of shifting somefing. "E lays an 'air across his toothpaste an' brush," Rosie told me. "So 'e'll know if yer've touched it."

Charlie didn't share. What was his stayed in his room. He looked after number one. Full stop. Bit of a loner, I heard people say. Never said much either, 'cept when he'd had a drink. Thought he was King Kong then. Us kids learnt quickly, an' kept out of his way.

The pawn shop in Merrow Street, off the Walworth road, had three gold balls hanging above it's door. It was a place that only the desperate entered. Mum got a few pound for her boys 'as new' clothes. If the money wasn't paid back by the due date, the pawn broker sold the gear on. Mum's wedding ring was in an' out of that place like a fart in a colander, until one day the ring just disappeared for good.

How Charlie didn't find out that his clothes had bin for a holiday, I'll never know. Maybe he did, an' I just wasn't around for the fireworks? Anyway, his gear had a few regular trips to Merrow Street after that. I fink they had more outings than he did!

—The Money Lender.—

There were a few ways to get money on the quick, an' mum, like a lot of locals, had used 'em all. Old Mrs Masters in the flats across the way, was offen a last resort. A loaded money-lender with a face like a worn out boot. "It's wicked the interest she charges, said Mum. "Shouldn't be allowed."

The cushion on the old girls armchair was lumpier than tinned rice pudding. "It's where she stashes all her money," said me friend. Our faces pressed against the window, trying to spy through the dirt an' the net curtain. "Sleeps there too, I bet," she said.

Mrs Masters was a moany old ratbag, always nagging us kids to stay off the grass, like it was her own private garden. As much as we wanted to, Mum said we weren't to give her any lip. No backchat. Had to keep her sweet, just incase! It wasn't easy, but we tried our hardest. Sometimes fings just flew out your mouth when you weren't even finking. Wasn't our fault.

"She's a bit like liquid paraffin," Mum told me. "It's the last fing yer want but it 'elps yer out now an' then."

Provident Man

When me an' rosie woke dad from his afternoon kip by waving a provident cheque in his face, he pushed it straight back at us. "Go an' treat yerselves," he winked, an' rolled over. We didn't need telling twice. We were out that door quick as a flash, before he remembered the suit he was s'posed to buy for a family wedding.

The Provident man was a regular visitor to the flats, an' knew most people in the area. Sometimes, if we were a bit short of money we'd stay quiet an' hidden when he knocked, just incase he spied us through the window. "I'll pay him double next week!" Mum smiled. He never gave up easily. He'd offen call through the letterbox like we'd all gone deaf, cheeky sod. The cheques came in handy when you needed somefing special, an' they could be spent in most shops.

Rosie an' meself dashed off to Peckham to buy our first pair of Bell Bottom trousers. They were the best fings in the world. I loved 'em to bits, an' couldn't wait to show 'em off. Mum wasn't too excited when she found out. "Where d'yer get the money from then?" She asked.

"Dad gave us his cheque," we answered, all innocent like.

Without anuvver word, mum stormed along the passage an' into the back bedroom. We decided it best to make ourselves scarce, leaving mum an' dad to sort fings out. Rosie had a brain wave. We popped those trousers on an' legged it down the stairs. Could hardly take fings back once they'd bin worn!

Didn't seem fair somehow, me an' Rosie getting to wear the latest fashion, while all dad got was a bit of a coatin. He still got to go to the wedding though, an' looked every inch his usual smart self!

Playground Song

Bell bottom trousers
shirt of navy blue
I love a Sailor
an' he loves me too.
When we are married
our dreams will all come true.
Bell bottom trousers
Shirt of navy blue.

Homeworking.

"Drink yer tea up Clare," said mum's friend Jean. "Be stone cold in a minute." Mum carried on stuffing the mountain of envelopes with rubbish that no one would want.

"I'll just finish this pile," she said, without looking up. Mum had seen the budgie fly from it's cage across to the net curtain, dropping a poo in her tea on it's way. "Fink I'll get meself some water, she decided, abaht to leave the room.

Jean got up from her armchair. "Not drinking yer tea? She frowned. Give it here then. Waste not want not, an' all that." she said, lifting the saucer from the table. "

"But it's cold now. Ere, Let me make a fresh one," Mum insisted, trying to snatch the cup away.

"This'll be fine, don't fret"

Minutes later mum returned with her water. She noticed the empty teacup, every last drop, gone! "Yer feeling alright mate?" asked Jean, knowing her friend was never one to turn down tea.

"Just a bit queasy, that's all."

Homeworking meant endless hours of work for very little money, but every penny counted when fings were tight. Mum offen shared the work at Jean's house. Sometimes us kids would help out too. One of the projects was to partly make up light shades. With thin red strips of plastic we'd wind it tightly 'round the silver wired skeleton. I liked the smell of plastic, so didn't moan when asked to do me bit.

Me sister Rosie came over one time, she'd bin playing out with Jean's daughter. The two girls pounded up the stairs like they were wearing hobnail boots. Suddenly it went quiet, followed by a muffled scream. We all dived out into the passage. *My* family never knew why the bit of mat sat arf way up the stairs, till then. Rosie had fallen straight through the loosely covered hole an' into the pitch black coal cellar, ending up with a big gash on her leg. The scar became a trophy that she flashed at all of us, offen.

The favourite of all the homework was to fold an' roll the Christmas cracker hats into tiny little sausage shapes. We'd pop a 'lastic band on to stop 'em from unravelling then chuck 'em in a box. It took days to fill that box!

I offen thought abaht the smiles on the kids faces when they unrolled those hats on Christmas day. If we'd got a penny for everyone of 'em, we'd have bin the richest family in the street, probably.

Playground rhyme

Christmas is coming
the Goose is getting fat
please put a penny in the old man's hat.
If you haven't got a penny, a ha'penny will do,
if you haven't got an ha'penny, then Gawd
bless you.

─Runaway.─

An overnight stay in Exeter Police Station under the beady eye of a matron had not bin part of the plan. Neither were the five weeks that followed, locked up in a remand centre in Bristol. Everyfing had gone to pot. So much for wanting a few days off school.

The morning started cold an' wet. I should have bin in a maths class, but the lure of the boutiques at the Elephant an' Castle indoor shopping centre (the first in Europe) had me walking the length of the New Kent Road instead. I heard the car blasting its horn but took no notice until it pulled up alongside.

Me sister Rosie, her new boyfriend Alan an' me bruvver Alfie were off on a trip to Devon. I didn't have a clue where Devon was but it sounded an okay place to be. I opened the door, abaht to climb in. "No way," said Alan. "Yer're underage, yer'll 'ave the law after us." It didn't take much to wear him down. A few minutes later I was in the back with me bruvver. We hadn't gone very far when the car ran out of petrol. Alan pulled into a Council office parking area, nipped off an' returned a short while later with anuvver one. This smarter car had a full tank.

Alan had nice memories of the caravan park at Dawlish, that his parents took him to as a child. Every year for a whole week they did nuffing but enjoy 'emselves, lying abaht on the warm sand, paddling in the sea, ice-cream an' everyfing. Seemed like a different world to the one we knew.

I did go to the seaside once, on a day trip with me Mum, Rosie, Alfie an' me little sis Sandy. I enjoyed the train journey to Brighton. I was abaht seven years old. Mum turned the pages of a comic nestled in me lap, as the train chugged along. Our tin bucket an' spade made clanking noises in the carrier bag tucked under the seat. I had me yellow swimming costume on beneath me clothes to save time later, just hoped I didn't need a pee!. I don't remember being by the sea exactly, just the journey an' mum's happy, smiley face.

Dawlish was dark and deserted by the time we arrived. Not one shinning light in a caravan window, an' no one strolling along the seafront. It was *nuffing* like I imagined. The summer season had finished a couple of weeks before. All the holiday makers were probably back home warming their hands 'round a coal fire, all except us of course, sitting in a freezing caravan with not a cup of tea between us.

Alan's idea of fish an' chips soon brought the smile back to me chops. Me an' Rosie waited in the van, willing them to get a move on. I wondered abaht mum an' dad, whether they'd reported us missing to the Police? Probably not, more likely fankful for a bit of piece an' quiet. The boys returned empty handed. Everyfing from then on happened in a bit of a rush. We all bundled back into the car. No food to quieten the gurgling in me belly. With goose bumps the size of moth balls, me an' Alfie snuggled under the red check travel blanket found on the back seat. Rain still beating on the windows as we drove in silence 'round Exeter town centre, with no idea where we were heading.

Pulling up at traffic lights, the car was suddenly surrounded by the Old Bill. They came from out of nowhere. There were thousands of 'em, or so it seemed. Maybe mum an' dad had reported us missing after all? Me an' Alfie still clinging to the warmth of the blanket, were ordered out of the car an' escorted to the Police Station directly in from of us, Rosie an'

Alan following behind. Apparently stolen goods were found in the boot, which they reckoned Alan lifted to pay for necessities i.e. fish an' chips, which we never even got a whiff of.

The night spent in the station had me belly in knots. I could hear Rosie crying an' shouting from her cell, wanting to know what had happened to me. I wished they would go to her, tell her I was okay, but they ignored her for ages, letting her get more an' more upset, an' there wasn't a fing I could do abaht it. I never heard a peep from Alfie, he was probably stuck in anuvver part of the building?

Being underage, having just turned fourteen, I got shut in a proper room with a fold-up bed an' a smelly grey blanket. A pile of Red Letter magazines sat close by on a small table, which the Matron lady, brought in to guard me, slowly worked her way through.

The morning brought questions, photo's, fingerprints, more questions, an' more bleedin' photo's, once they'd realised that Rosie's hair had shifted an' that she was actually wearing a wig!

She thought it was funny that they hadn't noticed the clues beforehand. The three inch wide band holding the fing on for instance or the stray curl of her own, different coloured hair that had escaped an' rested on her forehead. "Yer should 'ave said yer wanted more pictures, I'd 'ave 'ad me 'air set." she grinned. Rosie was braver than me. She would offen come out with unexpected funnies, catch you off guard, but for a short while after, your head was filled with somefing ovver than worrying thoughts. She was a lot smarter than people realised.

They might not have bin impressed with me sister, but I was, an' it was good to see her smiling. Fing is, everyone knew that Rosie could take care of herself. She *was* tough but she was also a softie too. There were many nights back home that she wouldn't sleep unless I sang a couple of her favourite songs, or made up a story to tell.

We were separated again, an' the questions started over. The social worker got on me nerves. They brought him in to ask the same fings that I'd already answered twice, three times before! "Ow many more times for crying out loud. I 'aven't done anyfing wrong," I moaned.

The station had it's own courtroom upstairs. By ten o/clock we were all back together an' standing in front of the Judge. Placed on remand for five weeks at various centres, we were taken away to wait for transport. I felt really sorry for Alfie. He was going to Bristol too, but would be on his own. Me an' Rosie were heading for the same place, Alan, being that much older got sent to a young mans prison.

As a kid you weren't s'posed to like the Old Bill, it's just the way it was. For some, it was almost like they were the enemy, an' you were best off not telling 'em anyfing. The young PC John, who escorted us to Bristol, just happened to be the nicest, kindest, friendliest, an' best looking Copper in the world. I vowed to remember his name an' number forever.

The Lodge turned out to be an enormous old house, divided into two, one arf being for younger girls, where I shared a room with two ovvers. Rosie slept in the section for the sixteen upwards. That first night was the worst ever. I lay awake for hours in the dark. Me thoughts jumping from one fing to the next. I listened to the sound of a girl crying in a room close by. Quiet, tired sounding sobs, that carried on well into the night. No one came by to check on her. I later learned that she was in 'solitary' for acting up. I *never* wanted to see the inside of that place!

The L-shaped communal sitting room, although divided, allowed me an' Rosie to catch up with each ovver everyday. We weren't allowed to talk, but managed to pass notes back an' forth, hidden in books an' pencil cases. The room was different to what I'd bin expecting. There were armchairs an' settee's, flowery curtains an' carpet, an' one enormous wooden table where we did school work an' stuff.

We thought that Bristol girls had a strange accent, an' they thought the same abaht us. One girl was remanded for nicking a pencil while anuvver got locked up for staying out too late at night. Fank gawd we didn't live in Bristol! A member of staff, a tall, skinny woman with lips so finn that they nearly weren't there, hated our guts, an' would let us know every chance she got. She made a point of picking on me an' giving me all the dirty jobs she could find. I was an easy target an' she knew it. She wouldn't have got away with it with Rosie, she'd have soon told her where to get off.

The five weeks dragged by. On the morning of the court hearing back at Exeter, we got to dress in our own clothes again an' meet with Alfie an' Alan. We waited nervously for the Judge to make his decision. Surely we wouldn't get sent back to the Lodge long term, for being passengers in a stolen car. The Judge shuffled papers an' spoke lots, but the only words that stuck in me mind were, "With Christmas just a few weeks away, I'm going to send you home to your family. You will appear at your local court in January for sentencing." By lunchtime we were on a train back to London, with two plain clothes Policemen for company.

Never really knew what reaction to expect when we walked into the flat, we were just relieved to be home. Brian, our older bruvver, went mental an' gave us the hiding of our lives!

Fings soon got back to normal. Christmas came an' went, leaving nuffing much to fink abaht 'cept the court hearing. Couldn't help but feel nervous. Devon started out as an adventure of sorts, but ended up a bit of a nightmare. I didn't want to get locked up again. I wanted to stay home with me family, even promising meself that I'd go to school.

January 7th 1969. We made our way to Court. Sitting in a corridor along with ovver kids, all waiting for our names to be called. Dad was a bag of nerves too. It's a wonder he didn't wash his hands of us with the worry we caused. We filed quietly into the courtroom an' stood by the chairs placed at the front of the isle. Three people sat behind the bench, whispering non-stop while thumbing through our papers. Me stomach churning over an' over, dad, still fiddling with his flat cap an' ready to burst into tears any minute.

I almost forgot to breathe when the Judge started talking. Five long minutes later, he shared his decision, two years probation for each of us. I wanted to larf an' cry at the same time, but had to stay still an' quiet till we were told to go. Poor dad couldn't help himself, tears rolling down his face as he fanked the Judge. Dad had bin to hell an' back an' yet still managed a smile. We weren't the best kids in the world, but we weren't really bad neither. Dad loved an' stood by us always. That, in our book made him far better than any kid could wish for, an he was all ours.

NB. Alan was given a two year jail sentence.

─EVICTION─

It happened a few weeks before Easter time. The morning sunshine brought the mums out onto the balconies to peg out their washing. Windows and doors wide open, gulping in the fresh air, while kids did their climbing an' balancing tricks in the monkey park across the way.

Old Tilly Hardiman next door, had a young man visitor, which didn't escape the attention of nosey Nora along the landing, ears pricked, an' standing with arms folded over her big belly, having a nose as usual.

The day had started well, until the moment a lorry pulled into the square. Soon afterwards, Tilly came to our flat. Her boy Charlie standing behind with his pushbike resting against his legs. He was a strange one, never could work him out. People said his mind weren't right. A ten year old boy stuck in an adults body. Never played with us kids cos he was too big. so he did nuffing 'cept ride his bike.

His mum stepped into the passageway an' spoke in whispers to mine. They cuddled before Tilly turned to leave. "Ta-rah Clare," she said. Mum cried. They'd bin friends a long time, an' helped each ovver out on many occasions. Mum couldn't fathom why Tilly hadn't told her before. Somefings can't be shared, I heard. Got to do with pride I fink?

We looked over the balcony as they walked through the square. Charlie, tall as a lamp post, steered his bike round the block towards

East Street, with bulging carrier bags swinging from the handlebars. His old mum struggling alongside with her big cloth shopping bag, weighing heavy on her doll-like arm. She never looked back.

"Best keep out of the way now duck," said one of the Council men, storming past an' into the flat next door. A sudden crash made me jump out me skin.

"Sorry abaht that," said the worker. "Just slipped out me 'ands."

Charlie's pub mirror from Jacks, the second-hand dealer, lay in pieces on the floor. Bit by bit the flat was emptied, with everyfing thrown over the balcony onto the waiting lorry. Their treasures smashing an' splintering for all to see. Adults an' kids alike stood rooted. No one moved. No one spoke.

Come lunchtime the toffee apple man parked his bike in the place where the lorry had bin. Kids yelled up to their muvvers who, for the lucky ones had money thrown down wrapped in a hanky, while ovvers were simply ignored. "Gis a bite. I won't take a big one, 'onest," was a regular plea from one so-called friend to another. "Getcha own," offen came the reply. Everyfing was back to normal.

1969 was the year of change. Fings were happening, forcing us kids to grow up that much faster still!

Dad had packed up work some months back. He'd bin poorly for a long time, an' spent a couple of weeks in Guys Hospital. His baccy tin and Guinness bottles on the locker next to the water jug. I never did find out what the problem was, but it was somefing that would take him back to Hospital on a few occasions.

Mum meanwhile grew tired of the constant scrimping, of juggling air and maybes. She had all but given up. The Bedford Arms became her sanctuary, A place that reminded mum, an' ovvers from the neighbourhood, how it felt to smile. For a few hours she could wear a different face, live a different life, until the 'time' bell sounded and she found herself wearing just one glass slipper.

Mum an' dad were together, but not really. They hardly seemed to speak to each ovver anymore. I fink the age difference had a lot to do with it. Poor dad seemed really old compared to mum. The 'boys', Charlie, Brian an' Terry, didn't help matters neither. They never had time for dad cos he wasn't their real one.

Us younger kids were doing our own fing, fending for ourselves a lot of the time. Some days, me an' Sandy, worked at the local cleaners sticking tickets on clothes ready for collection. The lady would bung us a couple of bob each. Easy money.

Saturday's were different! If you wanted to work the stalls down the Lane you had to get there early. Crawl out that bed before you'd even got your eyes open. Two quid for the day, an' if you were any good, they'd asked you back for the Sunday.

With the summer holidays not a million miles away me thoughts turned to Billy. I'd loved him forever even though he rarely noticed me anymore. Always off bike riding with his mates, not much time for girls. Sometimes I'd make excuses to be in Kinglake Street just to catch a glimpse! Billy was special. Kissed me once or twice, that had to count for somefing, didn't it? Eventually though I gave up the daydream of being his girlfriend, bit of a lost cause. 'Sides, I heard he'd bin sneaking off to see a French girl, who'd come visiting some Aunt up the road. He was welcome to her.

"Work experience," announced the Teacher. "A taste of things to come," she smiled. Like we don't know what that's all abaht I thought. Of all the days I decide to show me face in school, why'd it have to be this one? Like I ain't got enough to be going on with? Aylwin School used to be a grammar until it joined forces with Laxon, now it was like any ovver but with one big difference, us Laxon girls still wore a navy uniform while the Alywin girls wore green. Easier for the staff I s'pose to spot the bright from the not so, maybe? We weren't really welcome there which suited me fine, since there were far better places to be.

I didn't want to learn science or algebra anyway, an' as for languages, well, I had enough trouble speaking me bleedin' own. Only one fing interested me, I wanted to be a singer like Lena Zavaroni on the telly. *My* stage was at the bottom of the stairs in the porch. Me mates would pay a pretend shilling to sit an' listen. Sometimes I'd lean against the balcony an' sing 'Somewhere over the rainbow' at the top of me voice, an' sounding every bit like Judy Garland, so Mum said.

Teacher handed round the list of unpaid scivvying options. "What about something like this Maggie?" she pointed, arf way down the page. "An old peoples 'ome?" I said, giving an upward nod. "Ardly a barrel of larfs," I mumbled to meself, but at least it wasn't too far to walk. "Yeah, all right. Put me down for that one then."

"Daft cow," said me sister Rosie. "Whatcha wanna do that for? Come in the factories with me, it's a great larf." Rosie had already worked in a few of the factories 'around Tooley Street. Jobs were ten a penny. Give the Swift's cheese one a try out in the morning, an' if that wasn't up to scratch, you could nip along to the Priory Tea one come the afternoon.

Somefing was going on at home. Rosie shared secrets, 'cept this time she knew as much as me. Nuffing. The whispers an' sudden silences among the adults was a dead giveaway, different to the usual carry on. Normally if something needed to be out in the open, then it was said, no messing.

Dad had a saying "Don't worry worry, till worry worries you." I tried not to fink so much, after all, we'd bin through rough times before how much worse could it be? Whatever trouble was brewing, as long as we stuck together, we'd get by.

Some evenings an' weekends I'd help out at Lena Fox House, home for elderly ladies off Grange road. Teacher would be *so* impressed!

I'd set the tables for tea an' bring the meals through, write letters and birthday cards, or just sit 'round and chat, it was a good place to be. Out back was a small chapel with a piano where the ladies sang hymns on Sunday mornings. I'd offen sneak in there when fings were quiet, an' try me hardest to magic up a tune on those keys.

"Can I work 'ere when I leave school in the summer?" I asked the Matron lady. She smiled. "You'd best check it with your mum first. We could only pay four shillings an hour."

Mum wasn't home. Rosie stood in front of the mirror which hung above the mantle shelf. Her legs looking like cornbeef, from being too close to the fire. The hair dye, staining her forehead blue, stank an' dripped onto the lino. "What's up with you, misery guts?" She said into the mirror. "Pass us that towel will yer?" she pointed to the table.

I was worried abaht what was going on in the family, but there was no point keep dragging it up. "Ere, you know that French girl that Billy fancies? She said me 'airs the colour of shit!"

"Fucking cheek," said Rosie. "'Ope you gave 'er a slap?"

"No, she 'ad 'er Aunt there. But I'll get her tomorrow."

Rosie's short hair style only used up arf the dye. "Want yor's done?" she teased. Her chestnut brown locks now resembled slimy strands of liquorice mashed into her head. "Go on then," I said. "But don't get it all over me bleedin' face." Arf hour later an' back at the mirror. Stunned. Twins! The ruined towel tossed in a bag for the ragman.

A week later Mum shared the secret. "We're moving out," She said, popping a circle of cardboard into the gas meter. Avoiding our stares, she set out the cups for tea. Us kids stood there, mouths gaping, unhinged. Then questions tumbled out like a gob-stopper machine gone barmy. None of 'em answered. "We're just leaving an' that's all there is to it." We had a week to sort the flat out an' look for somewhere else. "Don't say a word to anyone," She warned.

"But what abaht me mates?" I asked.

"No one, I said. D'yer'ear me?" The following days were really strange with everyone carrying on as normal. The 'boys' went off to their jobs an' still moaned like hell, if they came home an' there wasn't any food on the table. They sorted their gear into bags ready to move to their bedsits at New Cross. They hardly seem bothered at all, at least that's the impression they gave.

Why wasn't anyone trying to put fings right? Maybe they couldn't? No one seemed to be helping us. Even the rent man had given up trying to bash the door in. Everyday brought us closer to losing our friends, everyfing! Dad would have tried to sort it, but not even he could turn it 'round this time. The illness had come back an' he was stuck in Guys again. How will he know where we've gone to? Will he ever find us again?

Alfie was first to go, packed his carrier bag an' left to stay at a friend's house. Full of the usual cheek an' daring, he smiled, pretending that all was okay, but I knew different. Hiding his pain behind a grin became second nature. I'd never seen him cry. Too big for a kiss now, but still jumping those stairs a flight at a time. Disappearing into the night, I watched him from the balcony. *My* bruvver, the best in the world going off on his own. "Alfie," I called. He stopped an' smiled up at me. "What's up Water Melon?" Me bottom lip trembling, I wanted to say, beg, "Please don't leave," but I couldn't. I knew he had to go, make his own way, better now than later. "I'll be alright," he promised, as though reading me thoughts. "Now get back indoors."

With the boys off to their new homes it was just mum an' us girls left to face the music. 'Cept we'd be long gone by then.

We had a bit of a reputation for being a tough family. I was a fraud, most likely snivelling in some corner when bottle was handed out. I didn't want to go, none of us kids did. It wasn't fair. We'd done nuffing wrong!

I checked out the rooms, mum's stuff, me record player, the three stupid bird ornaments nailed to the wall, flying heavenward, going nowhere. Mum spent years putting this home together, some bits older than meself. She knew it would all be destroyed but never uttered a word. She did cry though, mainly on the inside. I could tell by the way her stomach did this throbbing fing. Sometimes I'd catch mum wiping her eyes. "You okay?" I'd ask quietly, scared that she might say no. Turning away, she'd answer. "Course I am yer daft aperff. Somefing in me eye that's all."

I cried in the bedroom, bucket loads. That pride wotsit hadn't touched me yet. Water Melon, that was me, by name an' nature. 45s spinning on the record player, given to me by the Collins upstairs, Princess in rags. Runaway. World without love, all written abaht me. My songs.

Forcing words through the tightness of me throat, I sobbed me heart out to the player like it was a best friend. Shared all me feelings. Secretly whispered how frightened I was an' scared too abaht me dad, that I might not see him again, ever! On an' on, until, curled on the bed, sleep crept up on me like the bogey man of old, an' switched off me finking.

Our last night together found us each with our own bag to fill. Busy rooting 'round for favourite bits of clothing, the door knocker went. I stood in the passageway smiling at Billy. "Yer fancy comin' out tomorrow?" he asked. "Could go to the Fair on Blackheath if yer like?"

I still loved him.

"Who's at the door?" called Rosie.

"Billy," I yelled back.

"Is that right?" she said sarcastically. "So what 'appened to the French girl then, yer know, the one with the shit coloured 'air?" I heard her larfing, an' tried me hardest not to join in. Trust Rosie to turn fings 'round just to make me smile.

"Take no notice," I whispered. "Okay, see yer tomorrow then," I lied, an' shut the door. I wanted to tell him goodbye, but I couldn't. I'd promised me mum.

"Whatcha go an' say that for?" I asked Rosie.

"Couldn't resist it," she said. "'Sides, yer still owe her one, incase yer've forgot."

I hadn't, just didn't seem important anymore.

It was difficult getting to sleep that night. Us kids cuddled up in the double bed, whispering an' trying to make plans. Mum came in extra early to wake us. "Get yerselves up, kettle's on," she said, pulling back the curtains. "We want to be out of 'ere by eight."

The scullery window looked out on the swing park below. The tatty roundabout just waiting for someone to push it into life. Me an' Sandy hid behind that fing many times, in a bid to get out of being sent to the shop. I watched for a while as grey smoke drifted lazily from chimneys of the flats. Walworth was stirring. Holding teacups between both hands for warmth, us girls huddled together on the settee. The green tiled fireplace lay cold an' bare, having bin cleaned yesterday along with everyfing else. The flat had never bin tidier. It was a quiet time, none of the usual shouting an' hollering an' fighting over biscuits. Mum gave the sideboard yet anuvver wipe down. "don't want people talking behind our backs," she said.

"So what if they do," said Rosie, harfheartedly. "It's not like we'll know abaht it."

"That's beside the point," said Mum.

I reached out to turn the wireless on. "Best leave it love, it's too early," said Mum. "Yer'll wake Mrs Hardiman."

"But Mrs …" I started an' stopped. Mum stood still. Her glassy eyes staring 'cept she wasn't really seeing anyfing. Then, quick as yer like she pushed her cleaning cloth deep into her pinny pocket and rushed out to the scullery. Rosie elbowed me in the ribs. "Now look what yer've done. Clever clogs."

Bags in hand, we waited on the landing while mum closed the street door for the last time. Standing in the square, a last hug an' a few more tears to see us on our way. Mum's brave face crumbling, we set off towards the Old Kent Road. We could have bin going on a trip to the seaside as far as anyone knew, but there was no fun waiting at the end of this journey. No larfing till yer belly ached an' yer got the dreaded hiccups. No special treats in store.

The main road was already busy with people rushing off to work. We stopped outside the pie mash shop, still closed for business. I peered through the window. No lights flashing on the jukebox. I could still see me an' me mates standing there just two nights ago, singing along with Del Shannon, like we didn't have a care in the world. Would they miss me? Would they watch our stuff being chucked over the balcony? Maybe they'd rescue me skates, keep 'em safe for…

We popped Sandy on a bus, first arf of her journey to Southend where she'd stay with Aunt Ann. She'd done the trip before, on school holidays. Her eyes red an' puffy from crying, staring back at us through the mud stained glass as the bus pulled away. Little hand waving an' waving, becoming smaller by the second. Gone.

No one had told Aunt Ann that she was abaht to get a lodger!

Mum an' Mary were going to Nan's in Suffolk. Four year old Mary never said a word. She hung on like grim death to the back of mum's coat, she wasn't abaht to be left behind.

Me an' Rosie would stay together.

"I best be making tracks," said Mum. "Yer sure you girls are gonna be alright?" Mum was broken beyond mending. Her thin pale face mapped out the pain that threatened to tear her apart. "We'll be okay," said Rosie. "We're sorted, don't you worry abaht us." Slowly, we moved apart, walking off in different directions.

"So, where we going then?" I asked.

Rosie shrugged her shoulders. "Lets get a cup of tea at the café and take it from there. Smile, make like it's alright," she nudged. "For mum's sake."

I smiled. "But what abaht tonight?"

Rosie gave no answer, because there wasn't one. Me heart sank.

Glancing back over our shoulders, twice, three times, desperate to hang on, scared to blink an' miss that last image. We waved goodbye to each other, to family, to a life that was an' would never be again…

Author's note.

Our family never got back together again, although we would catch glimpses of one another from time to time. Us young ones stayed in various places, mainly friend's homes, for varying lengths of time.

Social services eventually arranged for Rosie and myself to live with a lovely Christian family in a large house in Peckham Hill Street. This became home to several teenagers who found themselves out in the cold, so to speak, with nowhere else to turn.

Alfie remained with friends, while Sandy, determined to escape the clutches of Uncle Bill, left Southend, and was taken in by a family back in Walworth.

Mum and Mary remained together, moving from one temporary accommodation to another, while Dad lived from day to day, often finding refuge in shelters for homeless men, before finally ending up in residential care.

Dad died four years after the family eviction.